make it yourself

The Complete Step-by-Step Library of Needlework and Crafts

COLUMBIA HOUSE/New York

Editor: Mary Harding
Assistant Editor: Margo Coughtrie
Editorial Assistants: Sally Fisher/Maureen Paton
Consultants: Greta Barrett/Angela Jeffs (Sewing)/
Patsy North (Embroidery and Crafts)/
Frances Rogers (Knitting and Crochet)
Managing Editor: Nicholas Wright
Design Co-ordinator: Jan Churcher
Production Control: Sheila Biddlecombe
Editorial Director: Graham Donaldson

Distributed by Columbia House, 51 West 52nd Street, New York, New York 10019

Printed in U.S.A.

Introduction

Machine knitting is the answer for those of you who have more enthusiasm for large projects than time to tackle them. In Volume 18 of Make It Yourself, you will find patterns for machine-knitted garments that are guaranteed to have a really professional finish. You'll also discover some delectable summer tops to knit by hand for you and the children.

Fine crochet can look like lace as you'll see from our elegant white tablecloths, our flower pillow, and net curtains. Those experienced at crochet will find these designs very rewarding.

Whether you're off to the beach or the mountains, or whether you simply want to stay cool in the city this summer, you'll find something useful among the dressmaking designs in this volume. Also, for the outdoor life, there are canvas bags to sew, a tent or windscreen to construct, and padded cushions to adorn the garden furniture. With alfresco meals in mind, there are embroidered place mats and a picnic case with all you need for an open-air feast.

Finally, you can learn how to work macramé—the ancient art of knotting. It's very relaxing and, with our step-by-step instructions, you can't go wrong.

make it yourself

Contents   Page

How to use this book...

Selecting a yarn

In this series, we are introducing a new and easy way to identify the yarn used in our knitting and crochet features! You will find an actual-size, colored photograph of the yarn given with each set of directions.

Materials Required:

150 (200) gm or 6 (7) oz each of yellow and green, 50 gm or 2 oz blue [100 gm = 360 m or 390 yds]. Knitting needles size 4 (Am) or 10 (Eng).

At one time or another, you have probably suffered the disappointment of finding that the yarn specified in knitting and crochet directions is difficult to obtain or totally unavailable in your area. When this happens you are faced with the often impossible task of finding a substitute yarn. By matching a yarn against our photograph, you can choose a yarn of similar weight and texture from the range of yarns available in your store or favorite needlework shop.

This method is also helpful if you have yarn left over from other projects and you are unsure whether it is the proper weight or texture and whether you have sufficient yardage to finish a new shawl or pullover.

To help you determine the amount of yarn needed, we have also listed the yardage per skein for the yarn used. Most yarn companies give the yardage per skein in their sample books, and many shops have interchangeable yarn lists which give the yardages per unit weight. You will then be able to see whether you will need to make adjustments in the number of skeins required of the yarn which you have chosen.

Before you start to work the pattern, work a test swatch and match it against the Tension given in the directions (see the Tension Gauge instructions below). Adjust the needle or hook size if necessary. Any yarn which can be worked at the tension given in the directions can be used for that pattern.

Centimeters or inches?

The metric system of measurement is gaining greater use and acceptance, and some needlework and crafts equipment and materials are already sold by the metric weight and/or length. For your convenience, we have given all the weights and measures in both systems. NOTE: In some cases, the conversions are not exact. The measurements have been rounded to the nearest convenient or appropriate number.

Tension gauge

One key to successful knitting or crocheting is the tension! Each of our directions is based on the given tension gauge (number of rows and stitches to 10 cm or 4″).

To check your tension, work a test piece 12 cm or 5″ square in the stitch pattern. Make a cardboard template with a 10 cm or 4″ square cut out of it. Place the template over your swatch and count the rows and stitches. Compare the numbers with the tension gauge given in the directions. If your swatch has too few stitches and rows, work more tightly or use smaller equipment. If you have more than the number given, use larger needles, or hook.

Directions for the items shown can be used for any yarn of similar thickness and texture, providing you can achieve the proper tension.

Do not be upset if you find that you do have to adjust the needle or hook size. This does not mean that there is anything wrong with your knitting or crocheting. The needle and hook sizes given in the directions are an average, but by no means an absolute. There is great variation in the tension at which different people work, and you will even find slight variations in the tension of your work. On days when you are tense or tired, your knitting or crocheting will probably be a little tighter.

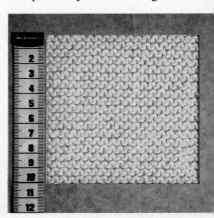

Fashion sizing

Dressmaking

Do you know your size? Don't just say 'yes', because as you already know, the fit of pattern and ready-to-wear sizes varies.

To eliminate confusion, we have lettered our sizes (A, B, C) instead of giving them the traditional numbering (10, 12).

Remeasure yourself and match your body measurements with those given in the chart below. All of the patterns are designed according to these measurements, so choose the pattern size which is right for your measurements. You may have to make minor adjustments in the pattern pieces to adapt them to your body contours, and Dressmaking Pattern Sheet 2 explains how to do this. Other dressmaking pattern sheets will deal with more complex fitting for specific garments such as pants.

DO NOT MEASURE THE PATTERNS. Every pattern includes, according to the design, an added measure to allow for easy movement when wearing the garment. Just compare your body measurements with the measurements given in the chart and choose the proper size.

Each pattern is given in five sizes. Two of the sizes are given on the pattern sheet and the other three sizes can be easily drawn from the two sizes given. Directions for adapting for the three additional sizes are given on each pattern sheet. Even if you are not one of the standard pattern sizes, but are a mixed size made up of several standard measurements, you can still use our patterns. Since each pattern can be adapted for five sizes – a size smaller, a size larger, and a size between the two sizes actually marked on the pattern sheet – it is possible to construct a pattern for yourself. Directions for constructing a mixed-size pattern are given on Dressmaking Pattern Sheet 2.

Knitting and Crochet

The knitting and crochet sizes are based on the Dressmaking Body Measurements Chart. For each direction, you will be given the actual body measurements for which the garment is intended. The finished knitted or crocheted garment will be larger than the given measurements to allow for comfort and movement.

Size: Directions are for 92 cm (36″) bust. Changes for 96, 100 cm (37½″, 39½″) bust are in brackets.

Do you know your size?

Don't just say 'yes'. Remeasure yourself, following the diagrams and instructions, and then check the Body Measurements chart.

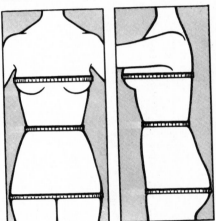

Bust – measure around the fullest part of the bust.
Waist – tie a string around your body so that it settles comfortably at your natural waistline. Measure your waist at the string.
Hips – measure around the fullest part of your hips (this generally falls 7″–9″ below your waistline).
Important hints:
When taking measurements, do not hold the tape measure slack or pull it too tight. The tape must lie evenly horizontal all around the body – it should not go up at the back and down at the front. You will find it simpler and more accurate to be measured by someone else.

Body measurements chart

WOMEN

Size	A	B	C	D	E	F	G	H
Bust	80 cm (31½″)	84 cm (33″)	88 cm (34½″)	92 cm (36″)	96 cm (37½″)	100 cm (39½″)	104 cm (41″)	108 cm (42½″)
Waist	59 cm (23½″)	63.5 cm (25″)	68 cm (26½″)	72.5 cm (28½″)	77 cm (30½″)	81.5 cm (32″)	86 cm (34″)	90 cm (35½″)
Hips	86 cm (34″)	90 cm (35½″)	94 cm (37″)	98 cm (38½″)	102 cm (40″)	106 cm (42″)	110 cm (43½″)	114 cm (45″)

MEN

Size	J	K	L	M	N	O	P	Q
Chest	84 cm (33″)	88 cm (34½″)	92 cm (36″)	96 cm (37½″)	100 cm (39½″)	104 cm (41″)	108 cm (42½″)	112 cm (44″)
Hip	88 cm (34½″)	92 cm (36″)	96 cm (37½″)	100 cm (39½″)	104 cm (41″)	108 cm (42½″)	112 cm (44″)	116 cm (45½″)
Neck	36 cm (14″)	37 cm (14½″)	38 cm (15″)	39 cm (15½″)	40 cm (15¾″)	41 cm (16″)	42 cm (16½″)	43 cm (17″)
Arm	60 cm (23¾″)	61 cm (24″)	62 cm (24¼″)	63 cm (24¾″)	64 cm (25¼″)	65 cm (25½″)	66 cm (26″)	67 cm (26½″)

CHILDREN

Size	S	T	U	V	W	X	Y	Z
Height	110 cm (43″)	116 cm (45½″)	122 cm (48″)	128 cm (50½″)	134 cm (52¾″)	140 cm (55″)	146 cm (57½″)	152 cm (60″)
Chest	60 cm (23¾″)	62 cm (24¼″)	64 cm (25¼″)	66 cm (26″)	68 cm (26¾″)	70 cm (27½″)	73 cm (28¾″)	76 cm (29¾″)
Waist	58 cm (23″)	59 cm (23¼″)	60 cm (23¾″)	61 cm (24″)	62 cm (24¼″)	63 cm (24¾″)	64 cm (25¼″)	65 cm (25¾″)
Hips	66 cm (26″)	68 cm (26¾″)	70 cm (27½″)	72 cm (28¼″)	74 cm (29″)	76 cm (29¾″)	80 cm (31½″)	84 cm (33″)

CMS
1 2 3 4 5 6 7 8 9 10 11 12 13 14 15 16 17 18 19 20 21 22 23 24 25 26

Two fine knits for summer

Fine knitting always arouses admiration, but most people are unwilling to tackle it because of the time and patience required. Knitting machines have changed all that, so here is a lovely summer dress to fire you with enthusiasm.

◀ The dress bodice has an openwork design. The opening has a crochet edge and loops to hold the buttons.

FOR BOTH

Size: Directions are for 88 cm or 34½" bust. Changes for 96 cm or 37½" bust are in brackets.

Materials Required:

[40 gm = 192 m or 209 yds]. <u>Dress:</u> 450 gm or 16 oz blue. 5 buttons. Buckle. Zipper: 25 cm or 10" long. <u>Cardigan:</u> 200 gm or 8 oz white. 7 buttons. <u>Both:</u> Crochet hook C.

Basic Stitch: Stocking or stockinette stitch.

Space Pattern: Transfer 1 st to next needle, leave spare needle forward, knit.

Tension: 30 sts and 38 R = 10 cm or 4".

Abbreviations: St(s) = stitch(es). K = knit. P = purl. R = row(s). Sc = single crochet.

DRESS

Bodice Back: Set R counter to 000. Cast on 132(142) sts and work straight for 100 R. In next R increase 1 st after the 7th st and before the last 7 sts, then repeat this increase R every 8th R 4 times. *At the same time,* after 104 R from beginning work 1 space after 4th st from each end (do <u>not</u> K 2 together beside it as this now forms an increase st.) Work 1 space in line with previous one on every 4th R 10(11) times — 164 (176) sts. Work straight until 148 (152) R in all.

Shape Shoulders: At beginning of every R, for 1st size cast off 3 sts 20 times, 4 sts 14 times; for 2nd size cast off 3 sts and 4 sts alternately 28 times in all and 5 sts 6 times. *At the same time,* when 176 (180) R have been worked, cast off center 20 sts; work on each side separately. In

every 2nd R at neck edge cast off 5 sts 2 times and 4 sts 1 time.

Left Front: Set R counter to 000. Cast on 66 (71) sts and shape side, armhole space increases, and shoulder to match Back. *At the same time,* when 92 R from beginning have been worked, work 1 R of 1 spaces in normal way beginning 20 (22) sts from front edge. Work 4 R, then over each of 1st and last space, work 1 space. Repeat last 5 R 1 more time. Work 4 R more, then work 1 R of spaces across R. *At the same time,* when 96 (100) R have been worked, decrease 1 st at beginning of next neck edge R, then 1 st every 3rd and 4th R alternately 23 times.

Right Front: Work to match Left Front, reversing shapings and pattern.

Belt: Set R counter to 000. Cast on 25 sts and work in K 1, P 1 rib for 560 R. Cast off.

Finishing: Pin out parts. Press with a warm iron over a damp cloth. Join seams, leaving 8 cm or 3¼" at lower edge of left side. Using crochet hook, work 84 sc around each armhole and work sc for 4 rounds. Fasten off, turn to wrong side and stitch down. Now work 72 (76) sc along straight edges of fronts, 62 sc to shoulder, and 48 sc across back neck; work 4 R of sc. Fasten off. For button loops, fasten yarn 4 (5) cm or 1½" (2") from lower edge of Right Front and make 6 ch, skip 4 sc, 1 slip-stitch into next sc, turn and work 13 sc around loop. Fasten off securely. Work 4 more loops along front about 4 cm or 1½" apart. Sew on buttons. Sew buckle to belt.

Skirt: This is worked sideways. Set R counter to 000 and cast on 180 sts. Work thus: * Work 14 R straight. Now place 168 sts from left side in holding position

Half-pattern for the bodice and one-tenth pattern for skirt in small (large) size. Numbers are centimeters; inches are given in the directions.

The basic pattern can be adapted very easily for this neat little sleeveless cardigan. Simply add a ribbed border at the waist and button the front rather more conventionally. It's easy!

and work over 12 sts remaining on right side. Now take 11 sts from holding position in every 2nd R 6 times, then 10 sts 9 times — 12 sts remain in holding position. Now work back by placing 10 sts in holding position in every 2nd R 9 times, and 11 sts in every 2nd R 6 times. Work 12 (16) R over all sts. Repeat from * 9 times more. Cast off.

Finishing: Join seams, leaving 16 cm or 6½" at top edge open. Sew skirt to bodice. Sew in zipper. Stitch a narrow hem at lower edge. Press seams.

CARDIGAN
Back: Set R counter to 000. Cast on 132 (142) sts and work 28 R in K 1,

P 1 rib. Continue as for Dress Bodice, adding the 28 R to each given number of R.

Left Front: Set R counter to 000 and cast on 66 (71) sts. Work 28 R in K 1, P 1 rib. Continue as for Dress, allowing for the 28 R.

Right Front: Work to match Left Front, reversing shapings.

Finishing: Press as for Dress. Work sc as for Dress, but work 92 (96) sc along straight edges instead of 72 (76) sc and work button-holes in the Right Front band in 3rd R over 4 sts (work 4 ch and skip 4 sc). Place 1st one 4 sts from lower edge, 7th one at beginning of Front decreases, and 5 more at equal distances between.

Shaping a flared skirt

The wedge-shaped darts which are worked to create the flare of a skirt, are made by shortening and lengthening the rows in a gradual and regular pattern. On the left side (waist), place the required number of needles in holding position. Then from right edge, work one row (right side row) over remaining stitches. *Before knitting back, wind the yarn around the first of the next group of needles in the holding position so that a connecting stitch is made. In the following right side row, bring the next group of needles into knitting position and work over them. The yarn around the needle is automatically worked together with the first stitch so that no hole appears. Repeat from the * until all needles have been brought back into knitting position. To shape the other half of the wedge, push the needles back into holding position in reverse order. Before every return row, wind the yarn around the last needle of the group in holding position so that no hole appears. Finally, work over all needles again.

This lovely rose-colored dress is not only elegant, but feminine. The diagonal lines of eyelets add interest to the bodice. The flared skirt is knitted from side to side.

Machine knitted in cotton

A knitted dress is always news

Size: Directions are for 96 cm or 37½" bust. Changes for 104 cm or 41" bust are in brackets.

Materials Required:

800 (850) gm or 29 (30) oz rose [50 gm = 150 m or 165 yds]. Set of double-pointed knitting needles size 0 (Am) or 14 (Eng). Zipper: 25 cm or 10" long. Bias binding.

Basic Stitch: Stocking or stockinette stitch.

Knitting Diagram: Only alternate rows are given. Work 1 row between each pattern row.

Tension: 30 sts and 40 R = 10 cm or 4″.

Abbreviations: St(s) = stitch(es). R = row(s). rnd(s) = round(s).

DIRECTIONS

Bodice Back: Set R counter to 000. Cast on 136 (150) sts and work in Basic Stitch, increasing 1 st each end of every 14th R 6 times — 148 (162) sts. Continue straight to 92 (88)

Shape Armholes: At beginning of every R, cast off 4 (5) sts 2 times, 2 sts 6 (8) times, 1 st each end of every 4th R 3 times, 1 st at beginning of next 4 R — 118 (126) sts. Work straight to 168 R.

Shape Shoulders: At armhole edge, for 1st size, cast off 4 sts at beginning of next 2 R and 5 sts at beginning of next 10 R; for 2nd size (cast off 5 sts at beginning of next 2 R, then 6 sts at beginning of next 2 R), 6 times. *At the same time,* when 172 R have been worked, cast off center 48 sts and work on each side separately. Cast off 2 sts at neck edge on every 2nd R 3 times.

Bodice Front: Set R counter to 000. Cast on 136 (150) sts and work 1 row. Now follow diagram from R 2, working this R thus: K 1 (edge st), then work from 7th (1st) st — 19th st 1 time, work repeat (20th–27th sts of diagram) 15 (16) times, K 1, then K 1 (edge st). Continue to follow diagram, shaping the sides and armholes to match Back; then work straight to 116 R.

Shape Neck: Divide work in center and work on each side separately. Decrease 1 st after the edge st at neck edge on every 2nd R until 30 sts have been decreased at this edge. *At the same*

time, shape shoulder to match Back after 168 R.

Sleeves: Set R counter to 000. Using a size smaller tension, cast on 84 (96) sts and work in K 1, P 1 rib for 46 R. Change to main tension and work in Basic Stitch, increasing 1 st each end of every 4th R 9 times — 102 (114) sts. Continue straight to 86 R.

Shape Top: At beginning of every R, cast off 4 (5) sts 2 times, 3 (4) sts 4 times, 2 sts 6 times, and 1 st 24 times, 2 sts 6 times, 3 (4) sts 4 times, 4 (5) sts 2 times. Cast off remaining 14 sts.

Finishing: Join shoulder and side seams, leaving 8 cm (3¼″) open at lower left side. Sew up sleeve, sewing lower 5 cm or 2″ on right side for turn-back. Sew in sleeves. Using the set of double-pointed needles, pick up and K 184 sts all around neck edge. Work 1 rnd in K 1, P 1 rib, then work 10 more rnds, but working 3 sts together at "V" on every rnd by slipping the center st and the st to the right of it knitwise, K1, and pass the slipped sts over. Cast off in rib.

Skirt: This is worked sideways in one piece. Set R counter to 000. Cast on 180 sts and work 16 R in Basic Stitch. *Place 174 sts on left side in holding position. K 6 sts on right, then on every 2nd R 9 times work over 10 more sts from holding position, then 12 more sts 6 times — 12 sts remains in holding position. Now place into holding position 12 sts in every 2nd R 6 times and 10 sts on every 2nd R 9 times more. Repeat from * 9 times. Cast off.

Finishing: Join seam to 17 cm (6¾″) from top. Join skirt to bodice, with opening at left side. Sew in zipper. Bind lower edge with bias binding. Turn up the hem to correct length and stitch in place.

▶ Here you can see the pattern on the bodice more clearly. The V-neck follows the eyelet lines and has a ribbed edging. A narrow belt completes the look.

Knitting diagram: Only alternate rows are given. Work one row between each pattern row. ▼

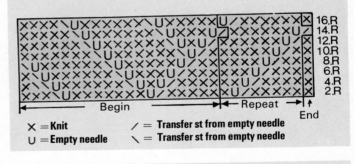

X = Knit
U = Empty needle
/ = Transfer st from empty needle
\ = Transfer st from empty needle

Half-pattern for the bodice and one-tenth pattern for the skirt in small (large) size. The numbers are centimeters.

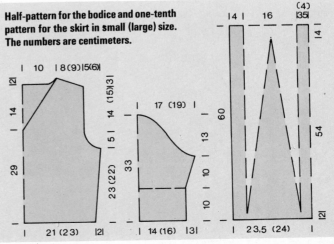

2191

Are you your own best friend? Spoil yourself with this soft and clinging dress for a smooth, flattering effect that will look good anywhere.

For experienced machine-knitters

Fluid and feminine

Size: Directions are for 84 cm or 33″ bust. Changes for 92 cm or 36″ bust are in brackets.

Materials Required:

870 (930) gm or 31 (33) oz [25 gm = 121 m or 132 yds]. Knitting needles size 0 (Am) or 14 (Eng).

Basic Pattern: Stocking or stockinette stitch.

Tension: 32 sts and 40 R = 10 cm or 4″.

Abbreviations: K = knit. P = purl. St(s) = stitch(es). R = row(s). St st = stocking or stockinette stitch.

DIRECTIONS

Left Back: Set R counter to 000. Cast on 160 (166) sts and work in st st for 16 R. Make a hem.

Work straight on right side (center back), but at side seam after 32 R decrease 1 st, then decrease 1 st every 40 R 9 times. *At the same time,* in the 32nd R, decrease within the R by

working together the 40th and 41st st, and the 100th and 101st st from center seam. Decrease within R on every 15th (14th) R 24 (26) times, staggering the decreases. Work straight until 408 R have been worked. Work should measure 102 cm or 40" including the hem.

If machine has a rib attachment, work in K 1, P 1 rib, but if not, transfer the sts to the knitting needles. In 1st R, work together every 2nd and 3rd st 33 (32) times – 67 (70) sts. Rib straight until 488 (496) R have been worked or 22 (24) cm or 8" (8¾") from yoke edge, ending at center back.

Shape Neck: At neck edge,

on every 2nd R cast off 23 sts 1 time, 3 sts 1 time, 2 sts 2 times, and 1 st 2 times. *At the same time*, when 492 (500) R or 23 (25) cm or 8½" (9") have been worked, shape shoulder at armhole edge by casting off 8 (9) sts 1 (2) time(s) and 9 (10) sts 3 (2) times.

Right Back: Work as for Left Back, reversing shapings.

Left Front: Work as for Left Back to 460 (468) R or 13 (15) cm or 5¼" (6") from yoke, then shape neck edge in every 2nd R by casting off 6 sts 1 time, 4 sts 2 times, 3 sts 2 times, 2 sts 3 times and 1 st 6 times. *At the same time*, shape shoulder at

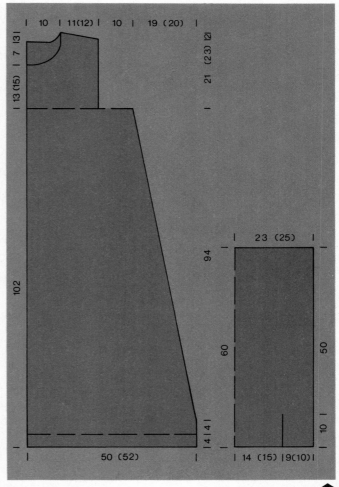

Here you see the dress without a belt. It falls in soft folds from the ribbed bodice to mid-calf length, thus allowing great freedom of movement.

Half-pattern for small (large) size. The numbers are centimeters; inch equivalents are given in the directions.

armhole edge to match Back, by casting off 8 (9) sts 1 (2) time(s) and 9 (10) sts 3 (2) times.

Right Front: Work as for Left Front, reversing shapings.

Sleeves: Set R counter to 000. Work slit in 2 parts. Cast on 29 (32) sts and work 40 R; leave sts in holding position. Cast on 119 (128) sts and work 40 R. Work across all sts — 148 (160) sts. Continue until 240 R have been worked. Cast off.

Work other sleeve with slit in reverse position.

Finishing: Press work lightly on wrong side. Join center seams neatly, joining fronts up to beginning of yoke. Join shoulders. Using knitting needles and a scrap of yarn, cast on 146 sts loosely (see How-to), then using original yarn, pick up and K 136 sts around neck edge, cast on 146 sts using a scrap of yarn — 428 sts. Work 2 cm or $\frac{3}{4}''$ in st st, beginning with a P R. Then K 146 sts, cast off 136 sts, K 146. Draw the scrap of yarn out of sts, and graft together the two sets of sts. Turn neckband in half to wrong side and sew down neatly.

Pick up and K 32 sts along each side of sleeve slits and work in st st for 1 cm or $\frac{3}{8}''$. Cast off. Sew down on wrong side. Join sleeve seams, then work tie ends and sleeve edging as for neck edge, casting on 80 sts with scrap yarn, then with original yarn pick up and K 60 (65) sts, then cast on 80 sts using scrap yarn. In 1st R, over sleeve edge sts only, work together 3rd and 4th st, then 6th and 7th st, then continue across these sts, thus working together every 3rd and 4th sts and following 2nd and 3rd sts — 203 (207) sts. Continue to match neckband. Sew sides neatly then sew in sleeves. **Press seams.**

Knitted-on ties

1 For knitted-on ties at a neck edge, cast on the required number of stitches with a scrap of yarn, using the simple loop method illustrated above.

2 Change to the original yarn and pick up the stitches around the neck edge. At the other end, cast on more stitches for the other tie with another piece of scrap yarn.

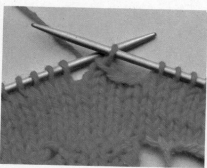

3 Work for 2 cm or $\frac{3}{4}''$ in stocking or stockinette stitch, then cast off the stitches around the neck edge. Place the tie stitches on spare needles and leave unworked.

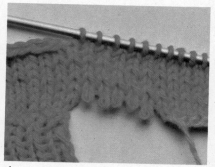

4 Draw out the scrap yarn at the beginning of each tie piece and place the released loops on needles. These stitches will now be joined to those at the other end.

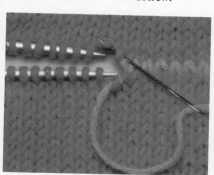

5 Place the needles for each tie side by side and with yarn in a tapestry needle, pick up 2 stitches, the first one from front to back, the second from back to front.

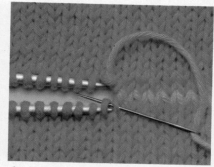

6 Take 2 stitches from the lower needle, from front to back and back to front. Continue, inserting needle in last stitch worked and taking 1 more stitch from needle.

Pistachio ice

Light summery colors look prettiest for this all-purpose striped top. It's knitted in one piece and has a straight neckline.

Size: Directions are for 84 cm or 33″ bust. Changes for 92 cm or 36″ bust are in brackets.

Materials Required:

175 (200) gm or 7 (8) oz green, 75 (100) gm or 3 (4) oz white [50 gm = 43 m or 47 yds]. Knitting needles sizes 1 and 2 (Am) or 11 and 12 (Eng). St holder.

Basic Stitch: St st.

Color Sequence: Alternately 8 R white, 16 R green.

Tension: 28 sts and 44 R = 10 cm or 4″.

Abbreviations: K = knit. P = purl. St(s) = stitch(es). R = row(s). St st = stocking or stockinette st.

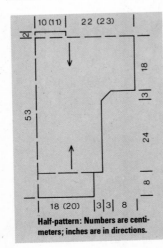

Half-pattern: Numbers are centimeters; inches are in directions.

DIRECTIONS

Front and Back: These are worked in one piece, beginning at lower edge of Front. Using finer needles and green, cast on 116 (126) sts and work in K 1, P 1 rib for 8 cm or 3″. Change to thicker needles and work in st st in Color Sequence to 32 cm or 12½″.

Shape Sleeves: *Cast on 1 st at beginning of next 2 R and 2 sts at beginning of following 2 R. Repeat from * 2 times more, then cast on 23 sts at beginning of next 2 R — 180 (190) sts. Continue straight until the 4th R of the 9th white stripe has been worked. In next R, K 62 (65), place next 56 (60) sts on st holder, cast on 56 (60) sts, and K last 62 (65) sts. Continue to work Back as for Front, but read cast off for cast on and decrease for increase.

Finishing: Go back to sts on st holder. Using thicker needles, white, and with right side of work facing, work in st st for 2 cm or ¾″. Cast off. Pick up and K 56 (60) sts along Back neck and work as for Front. Press work. Join side and sleeve seams. Turn in neck facings and stitch down. Turn in 2 cm or ¾″ at sleeve edge; sew down.

FOR ALL STYLES

Size: Directions are given for 88 cm or 34½″ bust. Changes for 96 cm or 37½″ bust are in brackets.

Materials Required:

[50 gm = 190 m or 207 yds.] Amounts are given in individual directions. Knitting needles size 1 and 0 (Am) or 12 and 14 (Eng). Circular needle size 0 (Am) or 14 (Eng).

Basic Pattern 1: See Pattern Charts A and B overleaf. Work right side R as given, with 1 st each end as edge st. P all wrong side R.

Basic Pattern 2: Stocking or stockinette st.

Tension: 27 sts and 44 R = 10 cm or 4″ over pattern.

Abbreviations: K = knit. P = purl. St(s) = stitch(es). R = row(s). Rnd(s) = round(s). St st = stocking or stockinette stitch.

CAP — SLEEVE TOP

Materials Required: 150 (200) gm or 6 (8) oz white.

DIRECTIONS

Back: Using finer needles, cast on 123 (135) sts and work 8 cm or 3″ in K 1, P 1 rib. Change to thicker needles and work in Basic Pattern 1 and Chart A. R 1 will read, K 1 (edge st) then 1st–3rd st, repeat 4th–9th sts to last 5 sts, work 4 sts as shown, K 1 (edge st). Continue in pattern, repeating the 10 R with 1 edge st each end until work measures 27 cm or 10½″.

Shape Armholes: At beginning of every R, cast off 3 sts 2 times, 2 sts 4 times, and 1 st 8 times — 101 (113) sts. Continue in Basic Pattern 2 to 34 cm or 13½″, then increase 1 st each end of next R and every 3rd R 13 times — 129 (141) sts. Work to 43 (44) cm or 17″ (17¼″).

Shape Shoulders: At beginning of every R, cast off 3

Tips for tops

Knit a pretty pullover or cardigan set for summer.

(3) sts 4 times, 4 sts 8 (4) times, 5 sts 2 (6) times, and 5 (6) sts 4 (4) times. *At the same time* at 45 (46) cm or 17¾″ (18″), cast off center 45 (49) sts and work on each side separately. At neck edge, cast off on every 2nd R 2 sts 2 times and 1 st 1 time.

Front: Work to match Back to 30 cm or 11¾″.

Shape Neck: Cast off center 55 (59) sts and work on each side separately. Work straight at neck edge, but continue to match Back for armhole and shoulder shaping.

Finishing: Join shoulders. Using finer needles and with right side facing, pick up and K 116 (124) sts along each armhole edge and work 4 cm or 1½″ in K 1, P 1 rib. Cast off in rib. Join side seams. Using circular needle and with right side of work facing pick up 60 sts from bac neck, 54 (58) sts from eac side front, and 60 (66) st from front. Work in K 1, P rib but decrease 1 st eac side of a K st at each fror corner on every 2nd Rn 4 times. Work 8 R more but increase 1 st each sid of the K st at corners o every 2nd Rnd. Cast off i rib. Fold bands in half t wrong side and stitch dow

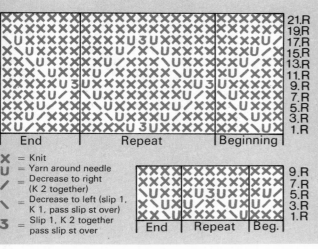

				21.R
				19.R
				17.R
				15.R
				13.R
				11.R
				9.R
				7.R
				5.R
				3.R
End	Repeat	Beginning		1.R

X = Knit
U = Yarn around needle
/ = Decrease to right (K 2 together)
\ = Decrease to left (slip 1, K 1, pass slip st over)
3 = Slip 1, K 2 together pass slip st over

			9.R
			7.R
			5.R
			3.R
End	Repeat	Beg.	1.R

CARDIGAN AND TOP

Materials Required: 150 gm or 6 oz white for each size for top and 250 (300) gm or 9 (11) oz for cardigan. 5 buttons.

TOP

Back and Front: Using finer needles, cast on 99 (111) sts and work 8 cm or 3″ in K 1, P 1 rib. Change

◀ **Charts for Basic Pattern 1. Chart B is above, Chart A is below. Right side R are given. Purl wrong side R.**

to thicker needles and keeping an edge st each end of R, follow Basic Pattern 1. Work from Chart A, working the 10 rows 5 times, then the 22 R of Chart B, and finally the 10 R of Chart A. *At the same time* increase 1 st in every 12th R 6 times — 111 (123) sts. When all patterns are complete, change to finer needles and work 4 cm or 1½″ in K 1, P 1 rib. Cast off in rib.

Straps: (make 2) Using finer needles, cast on 14 sts and work 35 cm or 13¾″

This second style is light and airy with brief straps and an attractive zigzag pattern broken along the top with a row of large diamonds.

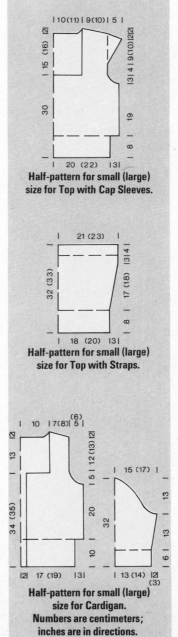

Half-pattern for small (large) size for Top with Cap Sleeves.

Half-pattern for small (large) size for Top with Straps.

Half-pattern for small (large) size for Cardigan. Numbers are centimeters; inches are in directions.

in K 1, P 1 rib. Cast off.
Finishing: Join side seams. Turn top ribbed border in half to wrong side and stitch down. Sew straps lengthwise to form a tube and sew in position.

CARDIGAN

Back: Using finer needles, cast on 123 (135) sts and work 10 cm or 4″ in K 1, P 1 rib. Change to thicker needles and work in pattern thus, working edge st each end throughout: 4 R st st, *10 R of Chart A, 22 R of Chart B, 10 R of Chart A, 18 R st st. Repeat from * and work straight in pattern to 30 cm or 11¾″.

Shape Armholes: At beginning of every R, cast off 3 (5) sts 2 times, 2 sts 6 times, 1 st 6 times, then 1 st each end of every 4th R 2 times − 95 (103) sts. Work straight to 47 (48) cm or 18½″ (19″).

Shape Neck and Shoulders: Cast off center 45 sts and work on each side separately. At neck edge on every 2nd R, cast off 2 sts 2 times and 1 st 1 time. *At the same time,* at armhole edge cast off 5 (6) sts in every 2nd R 4 times.

Left Front: Using finer needles, cast on 56 (63) sts and work 10 cm or 4″ in K 1, P 1 rib. Change to thicker needles and work pattern sequence of charts as for Back, working edge st each end. For 1st size, when using Chart A increase 1 st at beginning of R 1 and decrease 1 st at end of R 10; when using Chart B end after Repeat (for 2nd size, follow charts). Shape armhole and shoulder as for Back. *At the same time,* 34 (35) cm or 13¾″ (13½... cast off 22 (23) sts at fro... edge, then work straight this edge.

Right Front: Work match Left Front, but reverse.

Sleeves: Using fin... needles, cast on 100 (11... sts and work 6 cm or 2½... in K 1, P 1 rib. Change thicker needles. Decrease next R thus: K 5 (4), *K... K 2 together, repeat from... to last 5 (4) sts, K 5 (4)... 70 (76) sts.
Continue in st st, increasin... 1 st each end of every 10... (6th) R 5 (8) times − 8... (92) sts. Work straight... 19 cm or 7½″.

Shape Top: At beginning... every R, cast off 4 (5) s... 2 times, 3 (4) sts 2 time... 2 sts 4 (6) times, 1 st... (6) times, then 1 st eac... end of every 4th R 6 time... 1 st at beginning of next... (6) R, 2 sts 4 (6) time... 3 (4) sts 2 times, and 4 (... sts 2 times − 8 sts. Cast of...

Finishing: Join shoulder... Using circular needle an... with right side facing, pi... up and K 110 (116) s... along front edges, 28 s... along straight cast-off ne... edge, 56 sts to shoulde... and 61 sts from back ne... Work in K 1, P 1 ri... increasing each side of... K st at end of front edg... and decreasing 1 st eac... side of K st at beginning... straight neck edge on eve... 2nd R. Continue to 2 cm o... ¾″, then cast off 5 sts f... each buttonhole in next... casting them on again... following R. Work 1st on... 3 cm or 1¼″ from right fro... edge, 2nd one 3 cm or 1¼... away, and 3 more 9 c... or 2¾″ apart − measure... from beginning of butto... hole. Continue straight... 4 cm or 1½″. Cast off in rib... Join all seams, sewi... lower 6 cm or 2½″ of cuf... from right side to make tur... back. Sew on buttons.

And to co-ordinate with the second top, a matching short-sleeved cardigan with turn-back cuffs and a square neck. The diamond pattern is bordered with rows of zigzags.

In white cotton
Let's be brief

These brief and lacy little cotton tops are based on the camisole and are definitely for the young and liberated!

FOR ALL STYLES

Size: Directions are for 84 cm or 33" bust. Changes for 92 cm or 36" bust are in brackets.

Materials Required:

150 (200) gm or 6 (8) oz white [50 gm = 200 m or 220 yds]. Knitting needles size 0 and 1. Crochet hook size C.

Basic Stitch: Reverse st st with P side as right side.

Openwork Pattern: R 1: (wrong side) K 1, *K 2 together, yarn over needle, repeat from * to last 2 sts, K 2. R 2: P all sts and yarn-over sts. Repeat these 2 R.

Tension: 30 sts and 44 R = 10 cm or 4".

Abbreviations: K = knit. P = purl. St(s) = stitch(es). St st = stocking or stockinette stitch. R = row(s). Ch = chain. Sc = single crochet.

STYLE 1

Knitting Diagram: One pattern repeat is shown. Only the wrong side rows are given; all right side rows are purled. Work R 1–12 1 time.

Crochet Pattern: R 1: Join yarn at beginning of cast-off R, *3 ch, skip 2 cast-off sts, 1 sc into next st, repeat from *, turn with 3 ch. R 2: *1 sc in ch loop, 3 ch, repeat from * ending

Style 1: This may look complicated, but it's easy to work in reverse stocking or stockinette stitch and an openwork pattern.

The straps are in a simple rib. The eyelets are worked in rows or form little hearts. The openwork top band is crocheted.

Knitting diagram for Style 1: The diagram gives only the wrong side rows; purl all right side rows of the pattern.

	11.R
	9.R
	7.R
	5.R
	3.R
	1.R

1 Repeat

× = Knit
U = Yarn over needle
/ = Knit 2 together
\ = Slip 1, knit 1, pass slip st over
3 = Slip 1, knit 2 together, pass slip st over

1 sc in last ch loop, turn with 3 ch. Repeat R 2.

Back: Using size 0 needles, cast on 107(119) sts and work 2 cm or $\frac{3}{4}''$ in K 1, P 1 rib. Change to size 1 needles and work in Basic Stitch, increasing 1 st each end of every 14th R 6 times — 119 (131) sts. *At the same time,* when work measures 6 (8) cm or $2\frac{1}{2}''$ (3″) and ending after a P R, work 2 R of Openwork Pattern, then repeat it every 15th and 16th R 3 times, thus ending after a P R.

Work straight in Basic Stitch for 2 R. Now work the 12 R of Knitting Diagram, working 1st repeat from the 1st (4th) st, then repeat the 17 sts 6 (7) times more.

Work 2 R of Basic Stitch, 2 R of Openwork Pattern, then 3 R of Basic Stitch. Cast off, working 2 sts together at end of R as you cast off. Work Crochet Pattern along cast-off sts for 5 cm or 2″. Fasten off.

Front: Work as for Back.

Shoulder Straps: Using size 0 needles, cast on 8 sts and work 35 cm or $13\frac{3}{4}''$ in K 1, P 1 rib. Cast off in rib.

Finishing: Pin out parts, cover with a damp cloth, and leave to dry. Join seams. Sew Straps to Front, each 11 cm or $4\frac{1}{4}''$ from center Front; cross and sew them 8 cm or 3″ from center Back.

STYLE 2

Back: Using size 0 needles, cast on 107 (119) sts and work 2 cm or $\frac{3}{4}''$ in K 1, P 1 rib. Change to size 1 needles and increase 1 st each end of every 14th R 6 times — 119 (131) sts. *At the same time,* work in pattern thus: Work 2 R of Openwork Pattern, 2 R of Basic Stitch. Begin vertical holes in next R (wrong side): K 2 (8), *K 2 together, yarn over needle, K 15, repeat from * 5 times, K 2 together, yarn over needle, K 1 (7). Work 3 R in Basic Stitch. Work vertical holes on next and every 4th R and horizontal holes on every 24th R (every 6th vertical hole is in the horizontal R).

After the 5th horizontal R of holes, work 4 rows in Basic Stitch. Cast off, working 2 sts together at the end of R as you cast off.

Work 2 R of Crochet Pattern given for Style 1. Fasten off.

Front: Work as for Back, but after the 2nd R of crochet, divide work in center, leave center loop unworked and continue on each side separately.

Style 2: This version is also in reverse stocking or stockinet stitch, but here the eyelets are used to create squares. Note the crochet around the neck edge.

*Decrease by slip-stitching along to next ch loop, then work to last loop, 1 sc in loop and turn, repeat from * until 1 loop remains. Fasten off.

Shoulder Straps: See Style 1.

Finishing: See Style 1. Sew Straps to points at Front; cross and sew them 9 cm or $3\frac{1}{2}''$ from center Back.

STYLE 3

Knitting Diagram: The diagram shows the left half of Front and the center st. For right half, repeat from 1st st 1 time more. Note that the dots represent 55 (61) sts in P fabric on 1st R. On wrong side R, P the Openwork Pattern sts and yarn-over sts, and K the Basic Pattern sts.

Back: Using size 0 needles, cast on 109 (121) sts and work 5 cm or 2″ in K 1, P 1 rib. Change to size 1 needles and Basic Stitch; increase 1 st each end of every 10th R 6 times — 121 (133) sts.

Continue straight to 20 (21) cm or 8″ ($8\frac{1}{4}''$), ending after a P R. Now work 24 R of Openwork Pattern. Cast off.

Front: Work as for Back to 20 (21) cm or 8″ ($8\frac{1}{4}''$), ending after a K R. Now work from Knitting Diagram, remembering that there will be 55 (61) sts between the decreases in R 1. R 1 will read: *K 1, yarn over needle, slip 1, K 1, pass slip stitch over, P 55 (61), yarn over needle, K 2 together, repeat from * to last st, K 1. Work to end of R 24 of Knitting Diagram, then repeat R 25–32 until all the P sts have been decreased. Finish point as given and fasten off.

Shoulder Straps: See Style 1.

Finishing: See Style 1.

Style 3: Our third little summer top has a deeper rib and the border around the neck has been knitted with eyelets in an openwork pattern to create an attractive V-neck in the front.

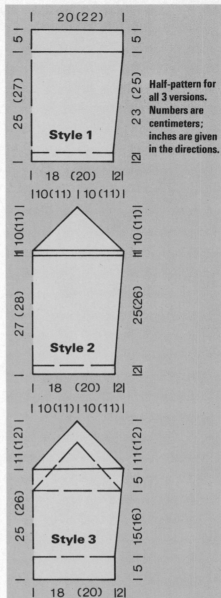

Half-pattern for all 3 versions. Numbers are centimeters; inches are given in the directions.

Style 1

20 (22) · 5 · 25 (27) · 5 · 23 (25) · 18 (20) · 2 · 10(11) · 10(11)

Style 2

10(11) · 10(11) · 10(11) · 10(11) · 27 (28) · 25(26) · 18 (20) · 2

Style 3

10(11) · 10(11) · 11(12) · 11(12) · 5 · 25 (26) · 15(16) · 5 · 18 (20) · 2

Style 3

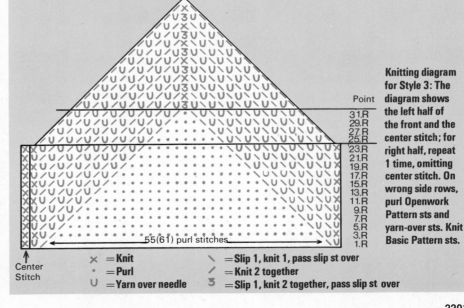

Knitting diagram for Style 3: The diagram shows the left half of the front and the center stitch; for right half, repeat 1 time, omitting center stitch. On wrong side rows, purl Openwork Pattern sts and yarn-over sts. Knit Basic Pattern sts.

Point

31.R
29.R
27.R
25.R
23.R
21.R
19.R
17.R
15.R
13.R
11.R
9.R
7.R
5.R
3.R
1.R

55(61) purl stitches

Center Stitch

× = Knit	\ = Slip 1, knit 1, pass slip st over
• = Purl	/ = Knit 2 together
U = Yarn over needle	3 = Slip 1, knit 2 together, pass slip st over

On the blue-and-white top, the honeycomb pattern is used as a band of decoration only. The rest of the top is plain.

Style 1

Soak up the sun

When the big heat is on, keep cool in our tiny halter-neck tops. They're feather-light with an attractive honeycomb pattern.

Size: Directions are for 84 cm or 33″ bust. Changes for 92 cm or 36″ bust are in brackets.

Materials Required:

Colors and quantities are given in individual directions. [50 gm = 202 m or 220 yds]. Knitting needles sizes 1 and 2 (Am) or 11 and 12 (Eng).

Basic Stitch 1: St st.

Basic Stitch 2: R 1: (rig side) K. R 2: P. R 3– Repeat R 1 and 2. R Repeat R 1. R 6: P *unravel next st dow 5 R, *with st at back work* take the 5 thread together with st, place left-hand needle and P, P Repeat from *, ending P instead of P 3. R 7–1 Repeat R 1–5. R 12: P *unravel st down 5 R before, P 3. Repeat from R 1–12 form the pattern.

Tension 1: 24 sts and R = 10 cm or 4″.

Tension 2: 22 sts and R = 10 cm or 4″.

Abbreviations: K = kn P = purl. St(s) = stitch(e St st = stocking or stock nette st. R = row(s).

Note: If making Style it will be advisable to wo a sample of Basic Stitch to note how pattern formed.

STYLE 1

Yarn: 100 gm or 4 white, 50 gm or 2 oz blue.

DIRECTIONS

Back: Using finer needle and blue, cast on 86 (9 sts and work 8 cm or 3″ K 1, P 1 rib. Change white and thicker needle and work in st st, decrea ing 1 st each end of eve 16th R 3 times — 80 (8 sts. Work straight to 2 (27) cm or 10″ (10¾″ Change to finer needles an blue and work 3 cm or 1¼ in K 1, P 1 rib. Cast off.

Front: Using finer needle and blue, cast on 86 (9 sts and work 8 cm or 3″ K 1, P 1 rib. Change thicker needles and st s and increase 1 st eac end of every 8th and 10t R alternately (every 10t R) to 98 (106) sts. Wo straight to 25 (27) cm o 10″ (10¾″).

Shape Armholes: At begi ning of every R, cast off sts 4 times and 3 sts times — 76 (84) sts.
Now work in Basic Stitc 2, working 36 R in patter and color sequence thus

1–5 white, R 6 and 7
[bl]ue, R 8–11 white, R 12
[a]nd 1 blue, R 2–5 white,
[R] 6–7 blue, R 8–11 white,
[R] 12 then R 1–5 blue,
[R] 6–11 white, R 12 then
[R] 1–4 blue. Continue in
[bl]ue on finer needles in K 1,
[P] 1 rib for 3 cm or 1¼".
[A]t the same time, **from
[b]eginning of pattern, de-
[cr]ease 1 st each end of
[e]very 2nd R 5 times (2 sts
[at] beginning of next 2 R,
[th]en 1 st each end of every
[2]nd R 6 times), 1 st each
[e]nd of every 4th R 10 (9)
[ti]mes. The 1st pattern R
[w]hich is R 6) will read:
[P] 2 together, P 1 (2), repeat
[fr]om * of pattern R, ending
[un]ravelled st as before,
[P] 1 (0), P 2 together. When
[rib] is completed, cast off.

[N]eckband: Using finer
[ne]edles and blue, cast on
[3] sts and work in K 1, P 1
[rib] for 65 cm or 25½".

[Fi]nishing: Join seams.
[Se]w narrow ends of
[ne]ckband to side edges of
[ba]ck rib, and stretching it,
[se]w to underarms at front.

[S]TYLE 2

[Y]arn: 100 gm or 4 oz white,
[5]0 (100) gm or 2 (4) oz red.

[C]olor Sequence: 5 R red,
[2] R white, 4 R red,
[re]peat from *.

[D]IRECTIONS

[B]ack: Using finer needles
[an]d white, cast on 86 (94)
[st]s and work in K 1, P 1
[rib] for 8 cm or 3". Change
[to] thicker needles and
[w]ork Basic Stitch 2 and
[C]olor Sequence, decreasing
[in] R 1 thus: K 2 (4), *K 2
[to]gether, K 12 (13), repeat
[fr]om * 5 times more —
[8]0 (88) sts. Keeping con-
[tin]uity of pattern, decrease
[1] st each end of every 30th
[R] 3 times — 74 (82) sts.
[W]ork to 25 (27) cm or 10"
[(1]0¾"), change to finer
[ne]edles and white; work
[3] cm or 1¼" in rib. Cast off.

[F]ront: Work rib and 1st
[de]crease R as for Back —
[8]0 (88) sts. Continue in
[B]asic Stitch 2 and Color
[S]equence, increasing 1 st

Style 2

each end of every 22nd
(24th) R 4 times — 88
(96) sts. Work straight to
25 (27) cm or 10" (10¾").
Shape Armholes: At begin-
ning of every R cast off 2
sts 4 times and 1 st 6 times.
Now work the decreases as
from ** of Style 1. *At the
same time,* at 33 (35)
cm or 13" (13¾") work 3
cm or 1¼" in K 1, P 1 rib.
Cast off in rib.
Neckband: Work as for
Style 1, but using white.
Finishing: See Style 1.

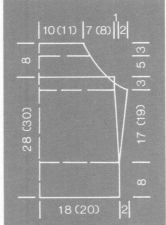

The red-and-white top is
patterned all over with
the honeycomb design.
The straps lie behind the
neck, leaving the back free.

◄ Half-pattern for small (large) size.
The numbers are centimeters; inches
are given in the directions.

If you're on the look-out for a stylish, easy-to-wear summer top, you'll love these two designs.

For Both

Size: Directions are for 92 cm or 36" bust. Changes for 100 cm or 39½" bust are in brackets.

Materials Required:

Colors and quantities are given in individual directions. [50 gm = 80 m or 90 yds]. Knitting needles size 2 (Am) or 11 (Eng). St holders.

Tension: 25 sts and 38 R = 10 cm or 4".

Abbreviations: K = knit. P = purl. St(s) = stitch(es). St st = stocking or stockinette st. R = row(s).

White Pullover

Additional Materials: 250 (300) gm or 9 (11) oz white, 100 gm or 4 oz blue. 4 buttons.

Basic Stitch: Reverse st st.

Color Sequence: *2 R blue, 6 R white, repeat from *.

DIRECTIONS

Front and Back: The pullover is worked in one piece, beginning at lower edge of Front. Using white, cast on 122 (132) sts and work 3 cm or 1¼" in garter st. Continue in reverse st st to 40 cm or 15¾".

Far and away the best

These two summer tops are variations on the same theme. They look equally attractive with or without a blouse underneath.

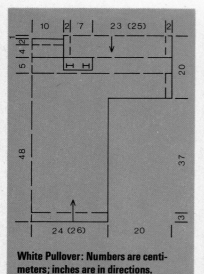

White Pullover: Numbers are centimeters; inches are in directions.

Green Pullover: Numbers are centimeters; inches are in directions.

Shape Sleeves: Cast on 50 sts at beginning of next 2 R — 222 (232) sts. Continue straight, but keep 5 sts each end in garter st and work to 44 cm or 17¼". Repeat the Color Sequence 2 times, then work 5 cm or 2" in blue, working buttonholes after 2.5 cm or 1". Mark the 66th–70th sts and 79th–83rd sts (71st–75th sts and 84th–88th sts) from each end, then in next R, cast off the marked sts. In following R, cast on 5 sts in place of those cast off. When blue band is completed, ending after a P R, cast off center 96 sts on next R for neck edge. Leave the 63 (68) sts on each side on st holders. Using blue, cast on 23 sts for Left Front underlap and, keeping 5 sts at inner edge in garter st, work in reverse st st for 3 cm or 1¼", then 1 cm or ⅜" in white, ending after a K R. Now K across 63 (68) sts of Left Front sts — 86 (91) sts.

Continue straight in reverse st st, keeping 5 sts each end in garter st and repeating the Color Sequence 2 times, then 3 R white. The Left Front is now completed. Work straight in Color Sequence for 1 cm or ⅜", ending at inner edge. Leave work on st holder.

Work Right Front to match, ending at inner edge, then cast on 50 sts and work across sts on st holder. Work in garter st over the 50 back neck sts and the 5 garter st border sts and work remaining sts in reverse st st for 2 cm or ¾". Then continue across all sts in Basic Stitch with garter st borders, matching Front stripe for stripe, and working shapings in reverse to end. Cast off.

Finishing: Join sleeve and side seams. Sew on buttons.

Green Pullover

Yarn: 300 (350) gm or 11 (13) oz green, 50 gm or 2 oz light green.

Basic Pattern: R 1: (right side) K. R 2: K 1 (edge st), P 5 (10), *K 10, P 10, repeat from *, ending P 5 (10) instead of P 10, K 1 (edge st). R 3–9: Work as sts present themselves. R 10: K. R 11: K 1 (edge st), K 5 (10), *P 10, K 10, repeat from *, ending K 5 (10) instead of K10, K 1 (edge st). R 12–18: Work as sts present themselves. R 19: P. Repeat R 2–19.

DIRECTIONS

Front and Back: The pullover is worked in one piece, beginning at lower edge of Front. Using green, cast on 122 (132) sts, work R 1 of Basic Pattern, repeat R 2–19 of Basic Pattern. *At the same time,* on R 2, join on 1 ball of light green at each end. In the 1st and last square of P 10 sts, work in contrast color. When R 10 is completed, alternate the contrast P square, so in R 11 the light green will be worked over 17th (2nd) st from each end. (Always remember at change-over of color to take the yarn along the 10 sts at back of work, catching in yarn after every 3 sts).

Continue thus, alternating the P squares in contrast color and keeping them in line to 40 cm or 15¾".

Shape Sleeves: Cast on 50 sts at beginning of next 2 R — 222 (232) sts, working extra sts into pattern so that the squares are a multiple of 10 and keeping 5 sts at each end in garter st throughout sleeves.

Work to 51 cm or 20", ending after a right side R. In next R, pattern 81 (86), K 60, pattern 81 (86). Repeat this R for 2 cm or ¾". In next R, pattern 86 (91), cast off center 50 sts, pattern 86 (91) sts. Continue separately on each set of sts. Keep the first 5 sts at neck edge in garter st and work to 60 cm or 23½", ending after a 5th or 15th R of pattern. The Front is now completed.

Now work Back. Work 1 cm or ⅜" straight on 1 set of sts, ending at neck edge. Work other set to match, then at neck edge cast on 50 sts, and work across other sts. Work the 50 sts and the inner garter st border in garter st for 2 cm or ¾", keeping all other sts in pattern. Then work across all sts in pattern and continue to match Front, ending with 3 cm or 1¼" in garter st. Cast off.

Finishing: Join all seams.

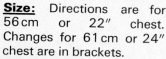

Size: Directions are for 56 cm or 22″ chest. Changes for 61 cm or 24″ chest are in brackets.

Materials Required:

100 gm or 4 oz for 1st size of long and short sleeve version and for 2nd size of short sleeve version. 150 gm or 6 oz for 2nd size of long sleeve version. Knitting needles and a circular needle size 2 (Am) or 11 (Eng). 5 buttons.

Basic Pattern 1: K 1, P 1 rib.

Basic Pattern 2: Reverse stocking or stockinette st (P side is right side).

Tension: 24 sts and 36 R = 10 cm or 4″.

Abbreviations: K = knit. P = purl. St(s) = stitch(es). St st = stocking or stockinette stitch. R = row(s).

DIRECTIONS

Back: Using blue or green, cast on 68 (78) sts and work in Basic Pattern 1 to 15 (17) cm or 6″ (6¾″). Change to Basic Pattern 2, beginning with a P R; work to 18 (20) cm or 7″ (7¾″).

Shape Armholes: Cast off 3 sts at beginning of next 2 R, 2 sts at beginning of next 4 R, and 1 st at beginning of next 6 R — 48 (58) sts. Work straight to 30 (33) cm or 11¾″ (13″).

Shape Neck and Shoulders: Cast off center 18 (24) sts and work on each side separately. At neck edge, cast off 2 sts on every 2nd R 2 times, and 1 st on next neck edge R. *At the same time*, at 31 (34) cm or 12¼″ (13½″), cast off 5 (6) sts at beginning of next 2 armhole edge R.

Left Front: Using blue or green, cast on 34 (39) sts and work armhole and shoulder to match Back, but always K the Front edge st to give a firm edge. Work straight to 25 (27) cm or 9¾″ (10½″), ending after a right side R.

Shape Neck: Cast off 14 (17) sts then work to end of row. Continue straight, matching Back at armhole.

Right Front: Work to match Left Front, reversing shapings.

Long Sleeves: Using blue or green, cast on 34 sts for both sizes and work 6 cm or 2½″ in Basic Pattern 1. Change to Basic Pattern 2 and increase 1 st each end of every 7th (6th) R 10 (12) times — 54 (58) sts. Continue straight to 26 (29) cm or 10¼″ (11½″).

Shape Top: Cast off 3 sts at beginning of next 2 R, 2 sts at beginning of next 6 R, 1 st at beginning of next 12 (16) R, 2 sts at beginning of next 6 R, and 3 sts at beginning of next 2 R. Cast off remaining 6 sts.

Short Sleeves: Using blue or green, cast on 48 sts

With picot edging

Tops for tots

Little ones will love these cardigans made in soft, fluffy yarns. Make them with long or short sleeves, depending on the season.

oosely and work 5 R in st st, beginning with a P row. **Picot R:** K 1, *yarn over needle, K 2 together, repeat from * ending K 1. Work 4 R in st st, beginning with a P row. Now using a fine needle, pick up sts along cast-on edge. Fold work at picot edge and P together 1 st from needle with 1 st from spare needle. Work to end. Continue in reverse st st, increasing 1 st each end of every 6th (4th) R 3 (5) times — 54 (58) sts. Work to 7 (8) cm or 2¾" (3¼").
Shape Top: Work as for long sleeve version.
Finishing: Press work with a warm iron over a damp cloth. Join all seams. For buttonholes, mark the place-

ment on the Right Front for a girl and on the Left Front for a boy. Place the first pin 2 sts from the lower edge, the 2nd one 5 (3) sts from the neck edge, and 3 more at equal intervals in between. *For the girl's cardigan*, with a circular needle and beginning at the lower Right Front, pick up 2 sts, *cast on 3 sts for buttonhole, skip next 2 sts, pick up 10 (12) sts to next pin, repeat from * 3 times more, cast on 3 sts, skip 2 sts, pick up 3 (1) sts to corner, 32 (38) sts to shoulder, 36 (44) sts from Back, 32 (38) sts to Front edge, and 60 (66) sts down other Front. *For the boy's cardigan*, with a circular needle and beginning at the

lower Right Front, pick up 60 (66) sts, pick up as for girl's cardigan at neck, then work down Left Front, following girl's directions for buttonholes in reverse.

Work as for short sleeve picot edge, working back and forth on the circular needle and beginning with a P R. Sew down on the wrong side. Sew on buttons.

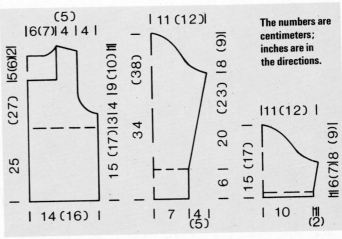

The numbers are centimeters; inches are in the directions.

2207

Playtime pullovers

The lovely openwork pattern makes cool-looking tops to wear with shirts and pants in spring and summer.

Size: Directions are for 61 cm or 24″ chest. Changes for 68 cm or 26¾″ chest are in brackets.

Materials Required:

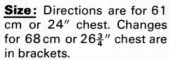

100 (150) gm or 4 (6) oz main color, 50 gm or 2 oz contrasting color [100 gm = 390 m or 425 yds]. Knitting needles and set of double pointed needles size 2 (Am) or 11 (Eng). Stitch holder.

Basic Pattern 1: Stocking or stockinette stitch (for Back).

Basic Pattern 2: See diagram. Only right side R are shown. All wrong side R and increased stitches are purled except first and last sts, which are knitted.

Border Rib: K 1, P 1.

Tension: 25 sts and 40 R = 10 cm or 4″.

Abbreviations: K = knit. P = purl. St(s) = stitch(es). R = row(s). Rnd(s) = round(s).

> Half-pattern for small (large) sizes: Measurements are in centimeters; inches are given in the directions.

The pattern chart gives only the right side or even numbered rows; the reverse side rows are all purled. ▼

DIRECTIONS

Back: Using main color, cast on 74 (90) sts and work 5 (7) cm or 2″ (2¾″) in Border Rib. Continue in Basic Pattern 1 to 17 (22) cm or 6¾″ (8¾″).

Shape Armholes: Cast off 3 sts at beginning of next 2 R, 2 sts at beginning of next 4 R, 1 st at beginning of next 6 (10) R − 54 (66) sts. Work straight to 31 (38) cm or 12¼″ (15″).

Shape Neck and Shoulders: Cast off center 24 (30) sts and work on each side separately. Cast off 2 sts at beginning of next 2 neck edge R, then 1 st on next neck edge R. *At the same time,* cast off 2 (3) sts on

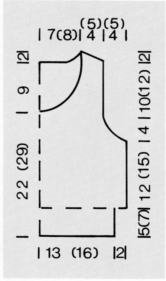

next 2 armhole edge R, 3 (3) sts on next armhole edge R, and 3 (4) sts on following armhole edge R.

Front: Work lower border as for Back, then continue in Basic Pattern 2. R 1 and every wrong side R: K 1, P to last st, K 1. R 2 (right side): K 1 (edge st), work across first 23 sts of diagram, repeat the next 8 sts of diagram 6 (8) times, K 1, then K 1 st for edge st. Continue to follow diagram with an extra st at each end for edge st, noting the change in R 14 where 1 st is taken from next repeat. R 1−16 form a complete pattern repeat.

Work armhole shaping to match Back and work to 22 (29) cm or 8¾″ (11½″).

Shape Neck and Shoulder: Cast off center 8 sts and work each side separately. Cast off 2 sts on next 4 neck edge R, 1 st on next 3 neck edge R, then decrease 1 st at neck edge on every 4th R 2 (5) times. At 31 (38) cm or 12¼″ (15″) shape shoulder to match Back.

Finishing: Join seams. Press. Using double-pointed needles and contrasting color pick up 102 (126) sts round neck edge and work 8 rnds in Border Rib. Cast off in rib. Work armholes to match on 90 (106) sts.

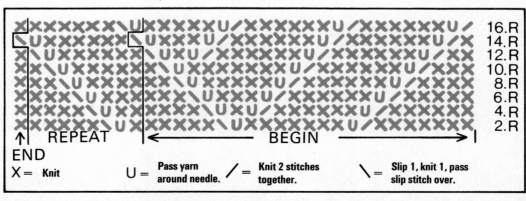

X = Knit	U = Pass yarn around needle. / = Knit 2 stitches together. \ = Slip 1, knit 1, pass slip stitch over.

Good sports

You'll find these pullovers quick and easy to knit. The red pullover has striped bands and collar, the other style is striped throughout. Each has a buttoned front opening.

FOR BOTH STYLES
Materials Required:

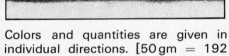

Colors and quantities are given in individual directions. [50 gm = 192 m or 210 yds]. Knitting needles sizes 1 and 2 (Am) or 11 and 12 (Eng). 3 buttons. St holders.

Basic Stitch: St st.

Tension: 23 sts and 32 R = 10 cm or 4".

Abbreviations: K = knit. P = purl. St(s) = stitch(es). St st = stocking or stockinette stitch. R = row(s).

RED PULLOVER

Size: Directions are for 58 cm or 23" chest. Changes for 62 cm or 24¼" chest are in brackets.

Yarn: 100 gm or 4 oz red, 50 gm or 2 oz each blue, green, yellow, navy.

Color Sequence: Cast on R and 1 R red, *2 R each green, navy, yellow, blue, and red, repeat from *.

DIRECTIONS

Back: Using finer needles and red, cast on 70 (74) sts and work in K 1, P 1 rib, in Color Sequence to 5 cm or 2". Change to thicker needles and, using red only, work in st st to 20 (22) cm or 8" (8¾").

Shape Armholes: At beginning of every R, cast off 3 sts 2 times, 2 sts 2 times, and 1 st 4 times — 56 (60) sts. Work straight to 33 (36) cm or 13" (14").

Shape Neck and Shoulders: Cast off center 18 sts and work on each side separately. At neck edge, in every 2nd R cast off 3 sts 1 time and 2 sts 1 time. *At the same time,* at 34 (37) cm or 13½" (14½") at armhole edge, in every 2nd R cast off 7 (8) sts 2 times.

Front: Work as for Back to 20 (23) cm or 8" (9").

Divide for Opening: Cast off center 6 sts; work on each side separately. Work armhole as for Back, then work straight to 29 (32) cm or 11½" (12½"), ending at opening edge.

Shape Neck: Cast off 3 sts at beginning of next R, then every 2nd R cast off 2 sts 2 times, 1 st 2 times, and 1 st every 4th R 2 times. *At the same time,* at 34 (37) cm or 13½" (14½"), shape shoulder as for Back.

Sleeves: Using red and finer needles, cast on 46 sts and work in K 1, P 1 rib for 2 cm or ¾". Change to thicker needles and work in st st, increasing 1 st each end of every 2nd R 5 times — 56 sts. Work straight to 6 cm or 2½".

Shape Top: At beginning of every R, cast off 3 sts 2 times, 2 sts 6 (4) times, 1 st 12 (20) times, 2 sts (4) times, 3 sts 2 times. Cast off.

Collar: Using red and finer needles, cast on 123 sts and work K 1, P 1 rib in Color Sequence for 10 cm or 4". Cast off in rib.

Finishing: Join seams. With right side of work facing, finer needles and green, pick up and K 30 sts from neck edge to beginning of neck division. Work in rib, working 1 R green, 2 R navy, 2 R yellow, 1 R blue; cast off in blue. Work other band to match, beginning from opening edge to neck edge and working 3 buttonholes in 2nd navy R, placing 1st one 1 cm or ⅜" from lower edge, and 2 more at 2.5 cm or 1" intervals. For each buttonhole, cast off 3 sts and in next R cast on 3 sts in place of those cast off. Sew on collar. Sew on buttons.

STRIPED PULLOVER

Size: Directions are for 66 cm or 26" chest. Changes for 70 cm or 27½" chest are in brackets.

Yarn: 100 (150) gm or 4 (6) oz navy, 50 gm or 2 oz red, green, yellow, blue.

Pattern: R 1: (right side) K 1 navy, *K 1 navy, K 1 secondary color, repeat from *, ending K 1 navy. R 2: P, alternating the colors.

Color Sequence: 2 R Pattern with blue, 4 R navy, 2 R Pattern with yellow, 4 R navy, 2 R Pattern with green, 4 R navy, 2 R Pattern with red, 4 R navy, repeat from *.

DIRECTIONS

Back: Using navy and finer needles, cast on 78 (82) sts. Work in K 1, P 1 rib, working 1 R navy, 2 R red, then in navy to 6 cm or 2½". Change to thicker needles and work in st st and Color Sequence to 24 (26) cm or 9½" (10¼").

Shape Armholes: At beginning of every R, cast off 3 sts 2 times, 2 sts 2 times, and 1 st 4 times — 60 (64) sts. Work straight to 38 (41) cm or 15" (16").

Shape Neck and Shoulders: Cast off center 18 sts and work on each side separately. At neck edge, in every 2nd R cast off 3 sts 1 time and 2 sts 1 time. *At the same time,* at 39 (42) cm or 15¼" (16½") at armhole edge, in every 2nd R cast off 8 (9) sts 2 times.

Front: Work as for Back to 25 (28) cm or 10" (11").

Divide for Opening: Cast off center 3 sts; work on each side separately. Continue to shape armhole as for

Back, then work straight to 34 (37) cm or 13½" (14½").

Shape Neck: At neck edge, in every 2nd R cast off 3 sts 1 time, 2 sts 2 times, 1 st 2 times, then 1 st every 4th R 2 times.

Sleeves: Using finer needles and navy, cast on 50 sts. Work in K 1, P 1 rib, working 3 R navy, 2 R red, 2 R navy. Change to thicker needles and st st and work in Color Sequence, beginning with red (green) for 1st stripe and increasing 1 st each end of every 2nd R 5 times — 60 sts. Work to about 6 cm or 2½", ending at same color as Back to armhole.

Shape Top: At beginning of every R, cast off 3 sts 2 times, 2 sts 4 times, 1 st 10 (4) times (then 1 st each end of every 4th R 2 times and 1 st at beginning of next 8 R). For both sizes,

at beginning of every R cast off 2 sts 4 times and 3 sts 2 times. Cast off remaining 12 sts.

Finishing: Join seams. Using finer needles, navy, and with right side of work facing, pick up and K 29 sts up right side of opening, 75 sts along back neck edge, and 29 sts down other side of opening. Work in rib, working 1 R navy, 2 R red, 3 R navy, and cast off in navy. *At the same time,* at neck corners, increase 1 st each side of corner st (always K the marked st on right side R), and in 2nd red R at left opening edge work 3 buttonholes, placing 1st one 1 cm or ⅜" from lower edge and 2 more at 3 cm or 1¼" intervals. For each buttonhole, cast off 3 sts and in next R cast on 3 sts in place of those cast off. Sew on buttons.

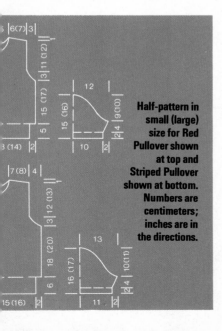

Half-pattern in small (large) size for Red Pullover shown at top and Striped Pullover shown at bottom. Numbers are centimeters; inches are in the directions.

2211

Stretch your imagination

Velour is a winner with everyone. And no wonder, as it's beautifully soft and versatile. These children's tops combine velour with knitting and are so comfortable that they won't want to take them off. The tops are made up of straight-sided pieces, so they're quick and easy to work.

BOTH STYLES

Size: Directions are for 68 cm (27") chest. Changes for 74 cm (29") chest are in brackets.

Materials Required:

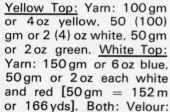

Yellow Top: Yarn: 100 gm or 4 oz yellow, 50 (100) gm or 2 (4) oz white, 50 gm or 2 oz green. **White Top:** Yarn: 150 gm or 6 oz blue, 50 gm or 2 oz each white and red [50 gm = 152 m or 166 yds]. **Both:** Velour: 0.50 m or $\frac{5}{8}$ yd. Sewing thread. Elastic thread. Knitting needles size 2 (Am) or 11 (Eng).

Basic Pattern: K 1, P 1 rib.

Stripe Sequence: (for Sleeves of Yellow Top) Cast-on and 6 R yellow, *7 R each of white, green, yellow, repeat from *.

Tension: 33 sts and 34 R = 10 cm or 4" (very slightly stretched).

Abbreviations: K = knit. P = purl. St(s) = stitch(es). R = row(s).

YELLOW TOP

Sleeves and Shoulder Yoke: Using yellow, cast on 100 sts and work in Basic Pattern and Stripe Sequence to 17 (18) cm or 6$\frac{3}{4}$" (7").

Cast off 24 sts at beginning of next 2 R — 52 sts. Continue straight to 28 (30) cm or 11" (11$\frac{3}{4}$"). Cast off 26 sts at beginning of next R and continue in white only for back yoke for 16 cm or 6$\frac{1}{2}$", ending at the cast-off 26-st edge. Now cast on 26 sts at beginning of next R and work as for other side, shaping by casting on instead of casting off and following stripes in reverse, thus ending with a yellow stripe. Cast off in rib.

Hem: (2 pieces required) Cast on 100 (110) sts in yellow and work in K 1, P 1 rib, working 6 R yellow, then 7 R each in green, yellow, white, and green. Cast off in rib.

Finishing: Cut out back and front from fabric, following the measurements on the diagram and adding 1.5 cm or $\frac{5}{8}$" seam allowances. Finish edges with zigzag stitch. Stitch back and front to knitted Sleeves/Yoke section. Join side seams. Join hem pieces and stitch on with a small, flat zigzag stitch, right sides facing and with shirring elastic on the bobbin. Turn under front neck edge and sew down.

WHITE TOP

Sleeves: Using white, cast on 100 sts and work in Basic Pattern for 6 R, then work (7 R red, 7 R white) 2 times. Continue in blue only to 30 (32) cm or 11$\frac{3}{4}$" (12$\frac{1}{2}$"). Cast off in rib.

Hem: (2 pieces required) Using blue, cast on 100 (110) sts and work in K 1, P 1 rib for 10 cm or 4". Cast off in rib.

Neck Border: Using blue, cast on 175 sts. Mark 28th, 60th, 114th, and 146th st with colored thread. Work in K 1, P 1 rib, working 2 sts together each side of marked st on next 8 R. Cast off in rib.

Finishing: Cut out back and front from fabric, following the measurements on the diagram and adding 1.5 cm or $\frac{5}{8}$" seam allowances. Finish edges with zigzag stitch. Stitch on sleeves and join side seams. Join hem pieces and stitch on with a small, flat zigzag stitch, right sides facing and with shirring elastic on bobbin. Join ends of neck edging. Turn fabric seam allowance at neck to right side and sew edging over it by hand.

The bright yellow top is made up of two rectangles of fabric stitched to the sleeves/yoke section which is knitted in one piece in rib.

The hem piece is stitched onto the fabric with elastic thread to pull in the width.

Inch equivalents	
	19 cm = 7$\frac{1}{2}$"
	20 cm = 8"
	25 cm = 10"
8 cm = 3$\frac{1}{4}$"	27 cm = 10$\frac{5}{8}$"
10 cm = 4"	28 cm = 11"
11 cm = 4$\frac{3}{8}$"	30 cm = 11$\frac{3}{4}$"
12 cm = 4$\frac{3}{4}$"	32 cm = 12$\frac{1}{2}$"
15 cm = 5$\frac{7}{8}$"	35 cm = 14"
17 cm = 6$\frac{3}{4}$"	36 cm = 14$\frac{3}{8}$"
18 cm = 7"	38 cm = 15"

On the white top, the sleeves, hem and neck edging are all knitted. The stripes on the sleeves are turned back to show them off. The hem piece is stitched onto the fabric with elastic thread as for the yellow top.

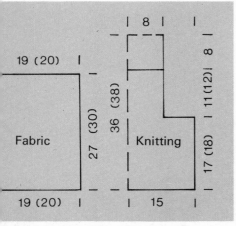

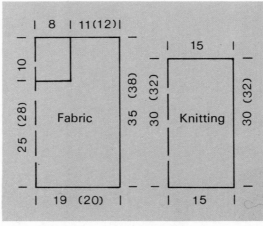

Half-pattern in small (large) size for Yellow Top, left, and White Top, right. The numbers are centimeters; inch equivalents are given opposite.

Crocheting the flower bands

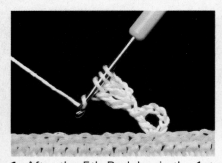

1 After the 5th Rnd, begin the 1st section with 5 ch, 1 tr in ch of previous rnd (to begin all other sections, work 1 tr, 1 ch, 1 tr in ch of previous rnd). To work 1st petal, make *4 ch, 2 half-finished tr in 1st ch, loop off together.

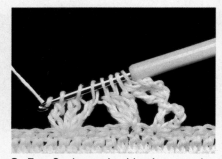

2 For 2nd petal, skip 1 st, make 3 half-finished tr in next st and keep all 4 sts on the hook, skip 5 sts, then begin the 3rd petal by making 3 half-finished tr in the 6th st, then yarn over the hook and draw through all 7 loops together.

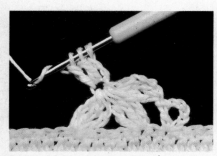

3 The 4th petal is not attached to the dc rnd and is worked as for the 1st petal, working the tr in the looped-off st of the previous 3 petals.

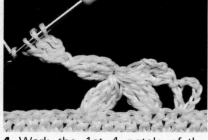

4 Work the 1st 4 petals of the next flower, working from the * of the 1st flower. Continue to work the flowers, remembering to begin each section with 1 tr, 1 ch, 1 tr.

5 In the next rnd, work the 5th and 6th petals. Begin rnd with 5 ch, 1 tr, then make *1 ch, work 3 half-finished tr in same loop as the 4th petal, yarn over and loop off together.

6 5 ch, then work the 6th petal as for the 5th petal.
Repeat from *, beginning each section as for previous rnd.
In the following rnd, work 1 dc in each st.

For the experts
Old world charm

This delicate lace cloth can be crocheted in any size by just adding more bands of net and flowers.

Size: 135 cm or 53″ in diameter.

Materials Required:

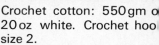

Crochet cotton: 550 gm or 20 oz white. Crochet hook size 2.

Basic Stitch: See Crochet Diagram. Shown is ⅛th of the first 2 flower bands of the tablecloth. Repeat Rnd 9–18, increasing as given in the directions.

Abbreviations: Ch = chain. Sc = single crochet. Dc = double crochet. Tr = treble. St(s) = stitch(es). Rnd(s) = round(s).

DIRECTIONS

Rnd 1: (right side) Make double loop round finger and in this loop work 3 ch (in place of 1st dc), 1 ch, *dc in loop, repeat from * 6 times more, then 1 ch, slip st in 3rd of 3 ch. Rnd 2: (wrong side) 1 ch for turn, 1 sc in 1st dc, 5 ch, *1 sc in next dc, 5 ch, repeat from * 6 times more, slip-st into 1st sc. Rnd 3: 2 ch for turn, *1 sc in center of the next space, 5 ch, repeat from * 7 times, slip-st into 1st sc. Rnd 4: Repeat Rnd 3. Continue by following the Crochet Diagram and the How-to photographs on left (these show how the flowers are repeated in

nds 16 and 17). The
wer rnds are increased
3 flowers on each of the
sections, the number of
below the flowers on
ch of the 8 sections must
ways be divisible by 8
us 7. The net rnds are
creased by 6 spaces each.
ork each repeat as
tched so that in the 1st
t rnd at each end of a
ction, 3 spaces are
orked over 3 dc, the
maining spaces over 4
. The center is therefore
ntinually increasing.
ter the 10th repeat of the
wer strip, work 1 rnd of
and fasten off.

**The circle is made up of eight
sections and each flower band is
increased by twenty-four flowers.**

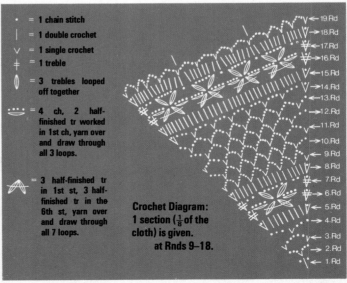

•	= 1 chain stitch
|	= 1 double crochet
∨	= 1 single crochet
‡	= 1 treble
	= 3 trebles looped off together
	= 4 ch, 2 half-finished tr worked in 1st ch, yarn over and draw through all 3 loops.
	= 3 half-finished tr in 1st st, 3 half-finished tr in the 6th st, yarn over and draw through all 7 loops.

**Crochet Diagram:
1 section (⅛ of the
cloth) is given.
at Rnds 9–18.**

←19.Rd
→18.Rd
←17.Rd
→16.Rd
←15.Rd
→14.Rd
←13.Rd
→12.Rd
←11.Rd
→10.Rd
←9.Rd
→8.Rd
←7.Rd
→6.Rd
←5.Rd
→4.Rd
←3.Rd
→2.Rd
←1.Rd

The age of elegance

This festive tablecloth is crocheted in an exquisite leaf and flower design. Display it in a prominent position on special occasions; it will look equally effective on both dark and light surfaces.

Size: 80 cm x 80 cm or 31½" x 31½".

Materials Required:

50 gm or 9 oz white cotton. Crochet hook size 3. **Leaf:** Make 16 ch. R 1: (wrong side). Beginning in the 2nd ch from hook, make 14 sc, 3 sc in last ch, then turn work and make 13 sc in other side of foundation ch. R 2: Turn without ch and work in sc. Beginning in the 2nd st, work in *back loops* of previous row and work 3 sc in center st of the 3 sc, then at end of R leave 1 st unworked. Repeat R 2, working 9 R in all. Fasten off.

Flower Motif: Make 6 ch and join into a ring with a slip st. Rnd 1: (right side). Work 1 ch, then 16 sc in ring, join with a slip st. Rnd 2: 7 ch for turn, *skip 1 sc, 1 hdc in next sc, 5 ch, repeat from * 6 times more, 1 slip st in the 2nd ch at beginning. Rnd 3: 1 ch for turn, *1 sc in hdc, (in 1st repeat, work in top of 2nd of 7 ch at beginning), 3 ch, 1 dc in center of 5 ch, then (5 ch, 1 slip st) 3 times in top of dc just worked, 3 ch, repeat from * 7 times more, 1 slip st in 1st sc. Fasten off.

Tension: 1 leaf square = 9 cm or 3½". 1 flower = 4.5 cm or 1¾".

Abbreviations: Ch = chain. Sc = single crochet. Dc = double crochet. Hdc = half double crochet. St(s) = stitch(es). R = row(s). Rnd = round(s).

DIRECTIONS

Make 4 leaves at a time and connect them when working the last R of 2nd, 3rd, and 4th leaves thus: make 1 ch, withdraw hook from loop and insert it in front part of relative stitch of adjacent leaf, draw loop through, and continue working. When working 4th leaf, join to 1st leaf to form a square. At end of 4th leaf, crochet the center of the leaves together neatly with the same thread by making 1 sc in the center of each leaf. Cut thread.

For the edging of each leaf square, attach thread to a leaf tip, *in the tip work 1 sc, 8 ch, 1 sc, **then work a picot of (6 ch, 1 sc in 2nd of the 6 ch, 2 ch), then 1 sc in next point of leaf. Repeat from **, working down leaf, across to adjacent point of next leaf, then to tip (9 picots between the leaf corners). Repeat from * 3 times more, ending with a slip st. Fasten off. 36 squares are needed in all and one square is joined to another when working the ch loop at top. To do this, only work 4 ch, withdraw hook from loop and insert into the ch loop of the adjacent leaf, draw loop through, and work remaining 4 ch. Follow photograph for arrangement. Now crochet the flowers,

joining them to the ch loops of the leaf edging in the last rnd. To do this, withdraw the hook from the loop and insert it in the appropriate place, a loop is drawn through, and 3 more ch sts are worked. The flowers and connecting lines, are shown on the diagram in color for the sake of clarity.

Flower 1: (pink lines). Join the center loop of the 1st point to the 3rd picot from a leaf tip, the 1st loop of the 2nd point to the 4th leaf picot, the center loop of 2nd point to the connecting points between the leaves, the 3rd loop to the following picot of next leaf, the center loop of the 3rd point to the next picot. Work the remaining 5 points without attaching them.

Flower 2: (turquoise lines). Join the first 3 points as for Flower 1, then work 3 points without attaching them. Join the 7th point to the 1st flower (at 5th point). For the 8th point, work only 3 ch for the center ch-loop, then work the connecting lines to the 1st flower and to the leaves thus: 1 picot (6 ch, 1 sc into 2nd of the 6 ch, 2 ch), 1 slip st in the

center loop of the 4th point of the 1st flower, 2 picots (omitting last 2 ch of 1st picot), slip-st into picot of the next leaf picot, 1 picot, slip-st into picot of following leaf, 2 picots (as before), 1 slip st in the 2nd ch of the flower point from which you began, then finish flower point.

Flower 3: (pale green lines). Repeat Flower 2.

Flower 4: (brown lines). Join the 1st 3 points as for the other flowers. With the center loop of the 4th point, work the connecting lines to the 1st flower (at 8th point), and join the center loop of the 5th point to the 7th point of 1st flower. Now, on the center loop of the 6th point, join the flower points in the center thus: make 1 picot and 1 slip st in the 6th flower point of each of 4 flowers. The center loop of the 7th point is joined to the 3rd flower (at 5th point), and with 8th point work the connecting lines to 3rd flower (at 4th point) and leaves, then back to 8th point. Fasten off. In this way, all areas between leaf squares are filled in with flowers.

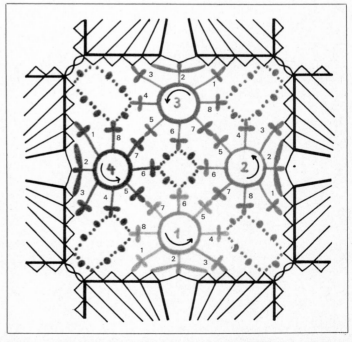

Above you see how the leaf squares are joined and the flowers are worked in the spaces between. The numbers give the snowflake sequence and the arrows indicate the direction in which to work each flower.

2217

In two motifs

For a pretty table

This fine tablecloth in white cotton may seem an old-fashioned idea, but the result is quite charming. Use it to protect the top of a beautifully polished table so that the surface can be seen through the pattern.

Size: 135 cm or 53″ square.
Materials Required:

600 gm or 22 oz crochet cotton in ecru. Crochet hook size C.
Basic Pattern: See How-to for Lace cloth motifs.
Tension: Square Motif measures about 9 cm or 3½″ along one side edge. Rosette Motif measures about 6 cm or 2⅜″ in diameter.

DIRECTIONS

121 Squares and 100 Rosette Motifs are required and these are joined together as the work progresses. First work 1 Square, then add the 2nd Square to it in last round, being careful that all squares are placed the same way. Add 3rd Square beside 2nd Square and then 4th Square to 3rd Square and 1st Square to form a large square. Crochet a Rosette Motif to Rnd 3. In Rnd 4, join it to center of the 4 Square motifs. The cloth is 11 Squares long and 11 Squares wide with the Rosette Motifs in between. The detail below shows the Motifs joined together.

This detail shows one Rosette Motif and four Squares when crocheted together.

2219

Lace cloth motifs

Abbreviations: Ch = chain. Sc = single crochet. Dc = double crochet. St(s) = stitch(es). R = row(s). Rnd(s) = round(s). Sp = space.

Square Motif

Make 18 ch. R 1 (right side): 1 dc into 6th ch from hook, *1 ch, skip 1 ch, 1 dc in next ch, repeat from * to end. R 2: 4 ch, *1 dc on dc, 1 ch, repeat from *, ending 1 dc into top of turning ch. R 3 – 5: Repeat R 2. Continue in rnds.

1 Rnd 1: 1 ch, **3 sc into corner sp, 3 sc in next sp, then in next sp work 1 sc, 5 ch, 1 sc.

2 Make 1 slip stitch into the sc before the 5 ch.

3 Into 5-ch loop, work (3 ch, 1 sc) 4 times, 3 sc in next sp, 4 sc in corner sp, then repeat from ** of Rnd 1 all around, thus working 8 sc in each corner sp and on longer side 3 sc into extra sp each side of center sp. Join rnd with a slip stitch into first ch stitch.

4 Rnd 2: 1 ch, *1 sc into 1st corner st of previous rnd (into center corner st on all repeats), 5 ch, 1 sc into the 2nd ch loop of small circle of previous rnd, 7 ch, 1 sc into the 4th ch loop of same circle, 5 ch, repeat from * ending with a slip stitch.

5 Rnd 3: 1 ch, then into every 5-ch loop work (3 sc and 3 ch) 2 times, then 3 sc. Into every 7-ch loop work (3 sc and 3 ch) 3 times, then 3 sc. Continue thus all around; join with a slip stitch.

6 Finish 1st motif, then join all other motifs to each other in Rnd 3. For this, draw hook out of loop after the 2nd ch of the center ch loop and insert it into a center loop

of the 1st motif and pick up the loop again, make another ch and finish the rnd. In joining, make sure that the crochet direction of centers is the same.

Rosette Motif

Make 6 ch and join into a ring with a slip stitch. Rnd 1: 1 ch, 15 sc into ring, join with a slip stitch.
Rnd 2: 6 ch, *skip 1 sc, 1 sc into next sc, 5 ch, repeat from * all around. Join with a slip stitch.

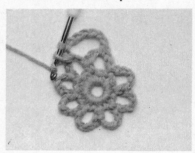

7 Rnd 3: Slip-stitch along to center of 1st loop, *1 sc into ch loop, 6 ch, repeat from * all around. Join with a slip stitch.

8 Rnd 4: (Join to center of 4 Squares) 1 ch, *4 sc into ch loop, 3 ch, 1 sc, 2 ch, draw hook out of loop, insert into the 3-ch loop from corner of the Square Motif and pick up loop again, 1 ch and continue with 1 sc, 3 ch, 4 sc. Join the next loop onto the following loop of the Square Motif. Repeat from *, connecting all loops to the Square Motifs. Join with a slip stitch and fasten off. Carefully weave in all ends and press the motifs.

Guipure lace

1 Stems: Work over filler strands. Fold the yarn to make a three-strand filler the required length, plus about 15 cm or 6″ for fastening off. Cover the three-strand filler closely with sc. By pulling on the filler strands you can make the cord thus created into various shapes.

2 Leaves and Petals: Work over a three-strand filler thus: 2 sc, 2 hdc, 9 dc, 2 hdc, 1 sc. Turn the piece and work on other side, crocheting over the three-strand filler between the stitches of the first side. Work 2 hdc, 9 dc, 2 hdc, 2 sc. Fasten off.

3 Work around edge in sc over another filler. On the Marguerite, all petals are worked as for the leaves, but they are joined together along the first and last 5 sc.

4 Harebell: Make 11 ch and work in sc, working 3 sc into last ch for the tip, turn piece; work along other side, but only to last st, leave this st and turn piece for next row.

5 Continue in sc, inserting hook into the inner thread of st only. Every R begins without a turning ch and into 2nd st and ends on the st before the last. Work 3 sc into the center of the 3 sc. Work as shown; at point make (10 ch, 1 sc) 4 times.

6 6-Petal Aster: Make 6 ch and join into a circle with a slip st. Rnd 1: With 3 ch as 1st dc, work

12 dc into ring, join with a slip st. Rnd 2: 3 ch as 1st dc, then (4 ch, skip 1 dc, 1 dc) all around, 4 ch, join with a slip st. Rnd 3: * 10 ch, turn and work 1 sc into 3rd ch, 1 hdc, 1 dc, 1 tr on each of next 5 ch, 1 sc into next dc of Rnd 2. Repeat from * all around. Rnd 4: This is worked behind Rnd 3. 2 ch, then 1 sc into the ch-loop of Rnd 2. Now work petals as in Rnd 3, but working the sc into ch-loops between petals. Fasten off.

8-Petal Aster: Make 10 ch and join. Rnd 1: Work 24 dc into ring, then work as for 6-Petal Aster.

7 Center: Make 5 ch and join into a ring with a slip st. Rnd 1: Work 3 ch as 1st dc, then (3 ch, 1 dc) 4 times into circle, 3 ch, join with a slip st. Rnd 2: In every 3-ch loop work 1 sc, 1 hdc, 3 dc, 1 hdc, 1 sc. Fasten off.

8 Scatter Flowers: 7 ch and join into a ring with a slip st, * 6 ch, 1 slip st into 1st foundation ch. Repeat from * 2 times.

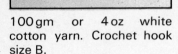

Crochet

For the experts only

A thing of beauty...

FOR BOTH

Materials Required:

100 gm or 4 oz white cotton yarn. Crochet hook size B.

SQUARE CUSHION

Size: 40 cm or 15¾" square.

Basic Pattern 1: R 1: 1 dc into 10th st from hook, *3 ch, skip 3 sts, 1 dc in next st, repeat from * to end, turn with 6 ch. R 2: 1 dc in next dc, *3 ch, 1 dc in 1 dc, repeat from * ending last dc into top of turning ch, turn with 6 ch. Repeat R 2.

Basic Pattern 2: R 1: 1 dc into 11th st from hook, *5 ch, skip 3 sts, 1 dc in next st, repeat from *, turn with 8 ch. R 2: 1 dc in 1st 5 — ch loop, *5 ch, 1 dc in next loop. Repeat from *, ending dc in top of turning ch, turn with 8 ch. Repeat R 2.

Tension: Over space pattern, 10 spaces and 12 R = 10 cm or 4".

Abbreviations: St(s) = stitch(es). Ch = chain. Tr = treble. Dc = double crochet. R = row(s). Rnd(s) = round(s). Hdc = half double crochet. Sc = single crochet.

DIRECTIONS

Back and Front: Work in one piece. Make 166 ch and work 45 cm or 17¾" in Basic Pattern 1. In next R work across 5 spaces and turn. Work straight on 5 spaces for 30 cm or 11¾". End yarn, work 5 spaces on other side to match,

then make 119 ch and work across first 5 spaces. Work in pattern across all sts (40 spaces) for 5 cm or 2". Fasten off.

Inset: Fasten yarn to an inner corner; work 3 dc into each space to end of side, turn and slip-st across the last 3 dc, turn, and work along next side, with 3 dc in each space. Continue thus along all 4 sides. Fasten off and mark corner with yarn. Fasten yarn at marked corner in 3rd dc up right-hand side of corner, 3 ch, 1 dc into 3rd dc to the left of the marked corner. Then continue from * of Basic Pattern 2 to last 6 dc at end of R, 5 ch, then slip-st to the 3rd dc up left-hand side, slip-st along to 3rd dc of next dc group, then continue in loop pattern across R just worked, ending 5 ch, 1 slip st into 3rd of next dc group on right-hand side. Continue thus, working in loop pattern and slip-stitching to side edges at end of each R until last R and then work thus: *2 ch, 1 slip st into corresponding place on top edge, 2 ch, 1 dc into loop. Continue across R, connecting top to loop pattern. Fasten off.

Flowers and Leaves: Make 3 stems of 7 cm or 2¾" and one each of 13 cm, 21 cm, and 24 cm or 5", 8¼", and 9½". Work 1 half Leaf with 12 cm or 4¾" Stem. Work 2 half Leaves and 9 whole Leaves, 1 Harebell, Scatter Flowers, 1 6-Petal Aster and 1 8-Petal Aster. (See How-to overleaf). Work 1 Small

Harebell thus: Make 6 ch and join into ring with a slip st. Rnd 1: Work 8 sc into ring. Rnds 2 and 3: 3 ch, 7 dc, join with slip st. Rnd 4: * 5 ch, 1 sc into 3rd of 5 ch, 1 hdc, 1 dc and 1 tr into next ch, then 1 sc into next dc of previous rnd, repeat from * 3 times more. Fasten off.

Finishing: Pin out cushion cover, dampen it, and leave to dry. Sew on stems, flowers, and leaves as shown in photograph. Fold cover in half, insert cushion, and join together with sc around all edges.

ROUND CUSHION

Size: 40 cm or 15¾" in diameter.

Basic Pattern 1: Rnd 1: 1 sc, * 4 ch, skip 2 sts, 1 sc in next st, repeat from * all around, join with slip st. Rnd 2: Slip-st to center of ch loop, 1 sc, *4 ch, 1 sc into loop, repeat from * all around, join with a slip st to top of 1st sc. Repeat Rnd 2.

Basic Pattern 2: See Square Cushion.

Tension: 8 loops and 13 rnds = 10 cm or 4".

DIRECTIONS

Back: Make 5 ch and join into a ring with a slip st. Begin all rnds with 3 ch as 1st dc, and end rnds with a slip st to top of ch. Rnd 1: 11 dc into circle (12 dc). Rnds 2 and 3: Work 2 dc in each dc. Now increase only in every 2nd rnd: In Rnd 5 increase in every 2nd dc, in Rnd 7 in every 3rd dc, in Rnd 9 in every 4th dc and so on until

diameter measures 30 c or 11¾". Change to Bas Pattern 1 and work un diameter is 40 cm or 15¾ working 5 ch instead 3 ch on last 4 rnds.

Front: Sketch a circle on paper with a diameter 30 cm or 11¾" and us this as a guide to form th circle shape. Make 41 c and work in R across th circle in Basic Pattern Increase at the beginnir

These two cushions are worked very cleverly to achieve the effect of Guipure lace. The motifs are crocheted separately and then sewn onto a trellis background so that they stand out in relief.

f the R with large turn-hain loops and at the end ith diagonal tr or dc. ecrease for top half by ip-stitching along loops. /hen circle shape is cometed, work all around the uter edges in dc, working dc, into each loop all round, then work in Basic attern 1 until diameter easures 40 cm or 15¾″, orking the last 4 rnds ith 5 ch loops instead of 3 ch loops. Fasten off.

Marguerite: Begin from center. Make 10 ch and join into a ring with a slip st. Rnd 1: 3 ch for 1st dc, (3 ch, 1 dc into ring) 9 times, 3 ch, slip-st to top of 3 ch. Rnd 2: (1 sc into ch, 3 ch) all around, join with a slip st. Rnd 3: *3 ch, 1 sc in next loop, 3 ch, 1 sc in next loop, 3 ch, 1 sc in same loop, repeat from * all around, join with a slip st —

15 loops. Rnd 4: Repeat Rnd 2.

Join petals on: * Work 1 sc around a three-strand filler (see How-to) and chain-st loop on Rnd 4. Continue working petals as shown in photos 2 and 3 of How-to, then work 1 sc into same ch in Rnd 4. Fasten off. Repeat from * 14 times with new filler strands. Make 10 Centers and 50 Scatter Flowers — see

photos 7 and 8 of How-to for directions.

Finishing: Press as for Square Cushion. Sew Marguerite to center of Front. Sew the Centers into center of the Marguerite. Sew on the Scatter Flowers as in photograph. Join Back and Front together with sc, leaving an opening for cushion. Insert cushion and close edges with sc.

Three edgings to crochet
Beautiful borders

For the prettiest windows imaginable, why not trim the edges of your curtains with one of three crocheted edgings, made in cotton.

Size: The edgings measure about 10 cm or 4" wide.

Materials Required:

Crochet cotton. These can be worked in various thicknesses but the amounts of cotton will vary from 35–50 gm per meter or 1–2 oz per yard, depending on the thickness. For our sample use a 3 crochet hook.

Basic Pattern: As shown in each Crochet Diagram.

Abbreviations: Ch = chain. Dc = double crochet. Sc = single crochet. R = row(s).

DIRECTIONS

Work a test piece first. Pin it out well in length and width and dampen it to judge the length you will require.

Edging 1: Follow Crochet Diagram 1. This shows the edging from the right side, so follow the diagram in the direction of the small arrows. At the end of R 4, begin first scallop thus: Make 6 ch. In R 5 work 1 dc into the last dc of the 4th R. In R 6 work 13 dc into ch loop, joining the last one with a slip stitch onto the last dc of R 4. Now work over the turning ch of R 3 with slip sts and work back in pattern as shown in diagram. In this way the scallop is enlarged up to R 9. Work R 10–15, then repeat from R 6.

Edging 2: The border is worked first in a straight strip in dc and ch and the pointed picot edge worked on one side later. Owing to the increases at the points, this edging has the appearance of a frill. Work from Crochet Diagram 2. Crochet the straight strip, repeating R 2 and 3 of diagram and follow the direction of the arrows. Then crochet the pointed edge, working in R. Note that the beginning and end of R are given, with the center repeated the number of times required.

Edging 3: Follow Crochet Diagram 3. This shows edging from the right side, so follow the diagram in the direction of the small arrows. Work to end of R 8, then make 14 ch and join with a slip st to R 6. Now make 2 ch and work 1 sc into turning ch of R 5. Work 24 dc in ch loop and join to R 9. Continue thus, increasing the scallop to R 13. Repeat R 2–13 as required.

Crochet Diagram 1: The diagram shows the edging from the right side, so follow the diagram in the direction of the small arrows. Begin to work the scallop at the end of R 4, enlarging it to R 9 as shown. Work R 10–15 as shown, then repeat from R 6 to work the next scallop as before.

*

Symbols for all diagrams

- • = chain
- ⌒ = slip stitch
- V = single crochet
- I = double crochet
- o = picot (4 chain, then 1 single crochet back into the first chain)

Edging 1: The band and scallops are worked together in one continuous piece

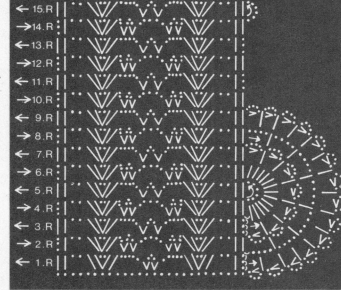

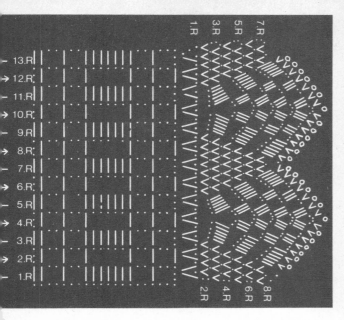

...ochet Diagram 2: First, crochet the ...aight band by repeating R 2 and 3 ...the diagram. The diagram shows ...edging from the right side, so ...low the diagram in the direction ...the small arrows. Then, crochet ...pointed edge, working back and ...th in rows. The Crochet Diagram ...ves the beginning and end of each ...w; repeat the center as many times ...required.

Crochet Diagram 3: The diagram shows the edging from the right side, so follow the diagram in the direction of the small arrows. Begin to work the scallop at the end of R 8, enlarging it to R 13 as shown. Work R 14–20 as shown, then work the next scallop as before, to length required.

Edging 2: The straight band is worked first, then the pointed picot edge is added.

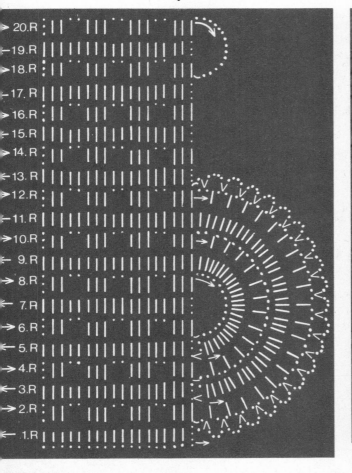

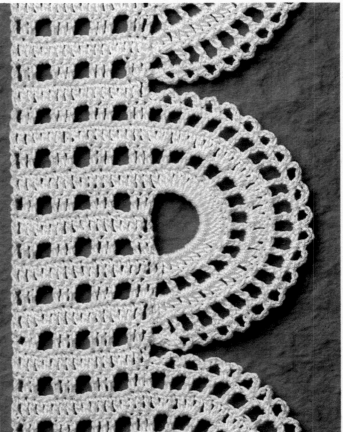

Edging 3: This design is worked as one continuous piece; see diagram left.

What's your hang-up?

Crocheted curtains have a charming, old-world appearance and create a cozy atmosphere in a room while letting the light filter gently through. These are worked widthwise in cotton yarn and can be made to suit any window size. The lower edge is fringed.

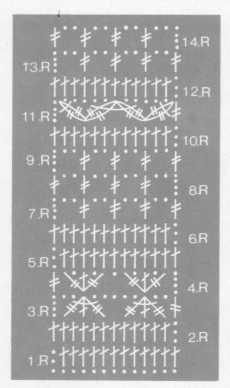

Crochet Diagram:
- † = **Double crochet**
- • = **Chain stitch**
- ‡ = **Treble**
- ⋏ = **1 treble, 1 double crochet, 1 treble looped off together**
- ⋏ = **2 trebles looped off together**
- ⋏⋏ = **4 trebles looped off together**

One repeat plus the beginning and ending sts of each row are given. Repeat rows 1–14.

Size: Each curtain measures 65.5 cm or $25\frac{3}{4}''$ wide and 62 cm or $24\frac{1}{2}''$ long (excluding fringe).

Materials Required:

125 gm or 5 oz white. Crochet hook size C.

Basic Pattern: See Crochet Diagram. Repeat R 1–14.

Tension: 30 sts = 10 cm or 4″. 1 repeat of pattern (14 R) = 14 cm or $5\frac{1}{2}''$ (measured before pinning out).

Abbreviations: Ch = chain. Dc = double crochet. Tr = treble. R = row(s).

DIRECTIONS

Work from side to side. For a 62 cm or $24\frac{1}{2}''$ length, make 183 ch and work in Basic Pattern. (30 repeats in width). Repeat R 1–14 4 times, then R 1–6 1 time. Fasten off.

Finishing: Pin out curtains and steam lightly. For insertion of curtain rod into upper edge, work 1 double tr and 2 ch into each R end. At lower edge, using 3 strands 6 cm or $2\frac{1}{2}''$ long, work a knotted fringe into each R end.

Pointed border

R 1: (right side) Make 28 ch. Beginning in the 4th st from hook, work in dc to last 2 ch, then work

2 half-finished dc, then loop off the 3 loops together. **R 2:** 3 ch for turn, 1 dc in 4th dc, 6 spaces in Basic Stitch, 1 dc in each of following 3 dc. **R 3:** 3 ch for turn, 1

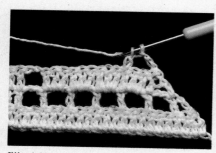

filled-in space, 1 empty space, 4 filled-in spaces, looping off the last dc with 1 dc worked in last dc of R 2. **R 4:** (photograph) 3 ch for turn, 1 dc in 4th dc, 2 empty, 1 filled, 1 empty, 1 filled space. **R 5:** 3 ch for turn, 1 filled, 1 empty, 1 filled, 1 empty space, with the last dc of this square looped off

together with 1 dc in the last dc of R 4. **R 6:** 3 ch for turn, 1 dc in next dc, 1 filled, 1 empty, 1 filled space. **R 7:** 3 ch for turn, 1 filled, 1 empty space, then R ends as R 5. **R 8:** 3 ch for turn, 1 dc in next dc, 1 filled space.

Now turn the work and for the next

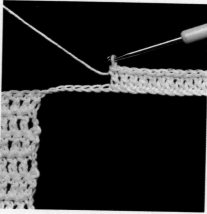

point make 21 ch and 3 ch for turn. For the new R 1, work 23 dc, working 1st dc into 4th st from hook.

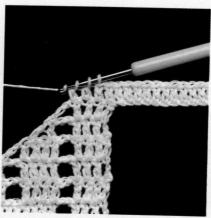

Now make 1 half-finished dc in the 2 last dc of R 8 and loop off these 3 loops together. Repeat from R 2. End last point with 1 turning ch and 1 dc into the last dc of R 8, and then fasten off.

Size: 110 cm x 94 cm
$43\frac{1}{4}$" x 37".
Materials Required:

Fine cotton: 350 gm or 1 oz white. Crochet hook C.

Basic Pattern: Ch an number of sts divisible by plus 7 for turn. **R 1:** 1 dc i the 8th st from hook, *ski 2 sts, 2 ch, 1 dc in next s repeat from *. **R 2:** 5 ch fo turn, 1 dc in next dc, *2 ch 1 dc in next dc, repeat fron *, ending with 2 ch and dc in 3rd turning ch. Repea R 2.

Crochet Chart: $\frac{1}{4}$ of the motif is shown. One filled in space consists of 2 d instead of 2 ch.

Tension: 13 squares of 3! sts and 14 R = 10 cm or 4"

Abbreviations: Ch = chain. Dc = double crochet St(s) = stitch(es). R = row(s).

DIRECTIONS

Make 434 ch and work in Basic Pattern for 1 R — 143 squares. Then at each end of next R work 2 dc in 2-ch space. In following R, work 2 dc in 2 dc at each end. Work in pattern to 12 cm or $4\frac{3}{4}$".

Now begin the motif, working the 2 dc over center space so that R 1 will read: 3 ch for turn, 2 dc in space, (1 dc, 2 ch) 70 times, 1 dc in next dc, 2 dc in center space, then work in pattern to end. Continue in pattern, following Crochet Chart. Work to center st, then work from 45th—1st st of Chart, then work in pattern to end. Work the 46 R of Chart then work from 45th R — 1st R. Continue in Basic Pattern as before to 91 cm or 36". Fasten off. Work Pointed Border as shown in How-to. Fasten off.

Finishing: Sew points to lower edge. Turn top edge to wrong side for 2 cm or $\frac{3}{4}$", stitch down. Pin out curtain and steam-press.

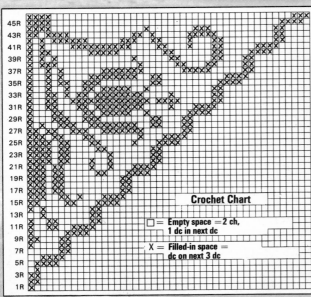

Crochet Chart

☐ = Empty space = 2 ch, 1 dc in next dc

X = Filled-in space = dc on next 3 dc

45R
43R
41R
39R
37R
35R
33R
31R
29R
27R
25R
23R
21R
19R
17R
15R
13R
11R
9R
7R
5R
3R
1R

Window dressing

Dress your window with a romantic lace curtain worked in filet crochet. The central floral motif is worked from the chart on the left.

On the shelf

Care for your kitchen in a creative way by crocheting delightfully old-fashioned borders for your shelves.

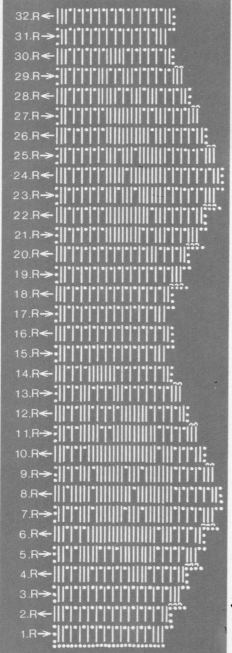

Materials Required:

A 50 gm or 2 oz ball of cotton makes about 100 cm or 39½'' of border.
Basic Stitch: See Crochet Diagram. 1 repeat of pattern is given. Repeat from 1st—32nd R and end length after R 15 or R 31. Follow Diagram in the direction of the arrows.
Tension: Across widest part, about 10 cm or 4'' (excluding edging).
Abbreviations: Ch = chain. Dc = double crochet. Sc = single crochet. R = row(s).

DIRECTIONS

Follow the Diagram, increasing for points at end of right side R by making 8 ch, turn. Slip-stitch along to 5th ch, then work 1 dc in last ch, which begins next R. Work· for length required, ending after R 15 or R 31. Fasten off.
For edging along points, fasten yarn in the last R of border at shaped edge. R 1: Work 1 sc in corner st, *3 ch, 1 sc in the last st of the next R, repeat from *, working 3 sc in the turning ch at outer point. Continue thus to end. R 2: Make 5 dc in each sc to outer point, then work 10 dc in center of the 3 sc. Continue thus to end.

◄ **Crochet Diagram: 1 repeat of the pattern is given. Repeat from R 1—32 and end after R 15 or R 31. Follow Diagram in direction of arrows.**

❙ = double   • = chain stitch   ∩ = slip stitch

69

Here comes the sun

Heatwaves are a feature of summer, so why not be prepared for the next one by adding several of these sun dresses to your wardrobe. In cotton or synthetics, the cut is flattering, the results sexy and sensational. You can make them all from Pattern Sheet 69.

Style 1

Style 2

Style 1 : (in sizes B and D) This halter-necked style has narrow released pleats to flatter the bust. The skirt has pockets in the side seams and is gathered gently into a wide waistband softened with a narrow tie belt. The detail above shows the back of the dress.

Style 2 : (in sizes A and C) The bodice of this second dress is cut like a pinafore dress and the straps cross at the back, buttoning onto the waistband as shown above. The skirt is gathered and has large patch pockets. Note that the dress wraps around at the back.

2233

Reinforcing shaped edges

It is useful to learn how to reinforce the edges of a pattern part so that the shape is retained. A halter-neck bodice that leaves the back bare is a good example, for the bias cut and curve of the sides would otherwise soon pull out of shape.

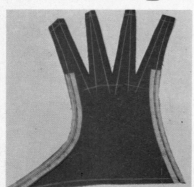

1 The illustration above shows one half of the front of the bodice. The neck strap is pleated to provide ample room for the bust. To reinforce the cut-out edges of the neck edge on the right, and the armhole on the left, cut two shaped strips 2 cm (¾") wide. Use non-iron, non-woven interfacing in the proper weight for your fabric. The strips should run the length of the sides up to the base of the pleats. Pin the strips to the wrong side of the fabric, then stitch down on the marked seamline.

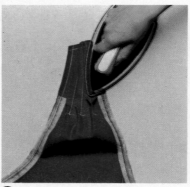

2 Pin and stitch the pleats, right sides facing, so that X lies on O. Secure the ends of the threads firmly. To flatten the pleats, begin by pressing the pleat seam allowances open, then press them sideways together. There is no need to finish the cut edges as they will be faced at a later stage.

3 Turn the bodice to the right side. Stitch and turn the strap, then press lightly. Pin the strap to the upper edge of the bodice, right sides facing, as shown above, then stitch in place. Note how the pleats release a soft fullness into the fabric. The bodice should now be faced.

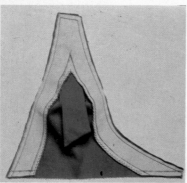

4 Iron a woven interfacing to the facing, then finish the inner edges as shown above. Pin the facing to the bodice, right sides facing. Stitch them together along the marked seamlines. Take care not to catch the strap into the stitching.

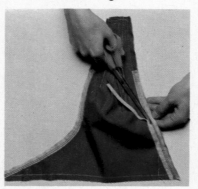

5 On the wrong side, trim the first strip of interfacing close to the stitching line as shown above.

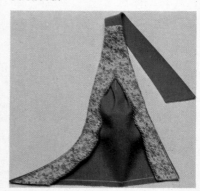

6 Turn the facing to the inside. Stitch the seam allowance to the facing, close to the edges, as far as you can. This will prevent the facing from turning to the right side and showing. Alternatively, top-stitch the edges. Press the bodice.

Style 3

Style 4

Style 3: (in sizes B and D) The style is simple, the effect is devastating, especially in black fabric. The simple, straight bodice is close-fitting with straps that cross at the back. The skirt is gathered onto the bodice slightly above the waist. There are pockets in the side seams and a zipper in the center back seam as shown in detail on the left.

Style 4: (in sizes B and D) Use a pretty print for this young-looking and romantic little dress designed specifically for teenage girls. Ruffles decorate shoulder straps that start at the waist and run over the shoulders to end in a point at the center back. The full skirt is gathered and there are pockets set into the side seams.

Summer bazaar

Style 1

Bedeck a belt
Make this wide belt by stitching strips of colored grosgrain ribbon onto a fabric base. It simply ties at the front with three ribbons as shown here and will be pretty on black or white summer dresses.

Smock a dress
Sew this dress for someone young and slim in sizes B or D. Make it dramatic in black cotton, then gather the bodice and pocket with shirring elastic and embroider the gathers with a simple herringbone stitch in lovely rich colors. Repeat the color scheme with buttons on the shoulders.

Style 2

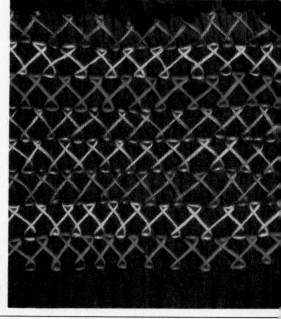

Revive a hat
Make a new summer hat, then enliven it with colored braid in bright shades stitched around the brim.

All these patterns
can be found on
Pattern Sheet 70.

Pick a purse

Small purses are a popular accessory these days, so why not make one for yourself. The purse illustrated is in black fabric, and the extra pocket on the flap is decorated with colorful ribbons. Bind the edges, add a button, and there you are.

Style 3

Style 4

Braid a blouse

Make a basic blouse in black, then decorate the front with grosgrain ribbon and braids. Pull out the threads at the ends then braid and tie them into tassels. The blouse is in sizes C and E.

Style 5

Summer bazaar

Sport a shirt

This stripey number is a classic man's shirt extended to hip length, making it perfect for beach wear. There are rounded slits and pockets in the side seams. The small collar is a stand-up style and the shirt buttons halfway down the front. Pattern is for sizes C and E.

Style 6

Style 6

Style 7

Relax in a robe

Make a beach or bath robe in size D or F. Plain towelling is easy to work with, but stripes are effective, especially when straight and bias cutting is combined. The yoke and sleeves are cut as one, there are pockets in the side seams, and the edges are bound with bias strips.

Bare a bikini

Bikinis are a vital part of any summer wardrobe, so make one in sizes B or D. The bikini top is worked double, the pants are cut on the bias.

Style 8

Style 11

Swing a cape

Here is a cape to provide an instant changing room on the beach. It is cut to make the best of the fabric, with the hood and main body cut as one. Bind with a contrast braid, then fasten with toggles down the front. The cape will fit all sizes from B to F.

Trim a towel and bag

Make a towel and bag to match your bikini for an outfit that's really "together"

Style 9

Style 10

Style 11

The bag is lined with plastic and fastened by means of two buttons.

Summer bazaar

Style 12

Style 13

Style 12

Base it on borders

These strapped dresses for mother and child are made up from large cotton scarves. The borders have been used for the straps and bodice, and whole scarves have been used to make the gathered skirt. You will need three scarves for the mother's dress (Style 12 in sizes B and D) and two for the child's dress (Style 13 in sizes S and U).

Choose an unusual fabric to set off the style. The pattern is given in sizes A and C.

Play up a print

This simple little cotton dress has a high waist, small sleeves cut in one with the bodice, and a calf-length gathered skirt.

Style 14

Style it
in scarves
You can literally
make this overtop
in less than
an hour — all you
need are two scarves.
The deep side
slits and roomy
sleeves make it a
very easy style
to wear. The pattern
is in sizes B and D.

Finally, just for
fun, make yourself
a bag to tie up
all your worldly
possessions.

Style 15

Baby bag

Have a go at patchwork and give your baby a bright and warm sleeping bag.

Materials Required:

Assortment of colored fabric scraps. Cotton fabric for waistband and shoulder straps: 0.30 m ($\frac{3}{8}$ yd), 90 cm (36") wide. Soft lining fabric: 0.75 m ($\frac{7}{8}$ yd), 150 cm (58") wide. Elastic: 0.75 m ($\frac{7}{8}$ yd), 0.5 cm ($\frac{1}{4}$") wide. Zipper: 35 cm (14"). Sewing thread.

Making the bag

Cut out all pieces with 1 cm ($\frac{3}{8}$") seam allowance. Cut out bag once in lining fabric, waistband once on the fold, and straps twice on fold to the measurements given on the diagram. Cut a template in cardboard for the patches in the form of a right-angled triangle with measurements as in the diagram. Two triangles joined on the diagonal form a square. Using the template, cut out 120 triangles in various fabrics, allowing 1 cm ($\frac{3}{8}$") all around for seams. Sort them into a pleasing arrangement of design and color and then sew pairs of triangles together into squares. Stitch together

6 strips of 10 squares each and sew the strips together as shown.
Place the patchwork piece onto the lining and baste together. Stitch together along the horizontal and vertical lines. Join the center front, leaving 35 cm (14") open for the zipper.
Now fold the bag, right sides facing, so that center front is over center back and stitch up the lower edge.
Before stitching the waistband to the upper edge, make a 8 cm (3") dart on each side of back and front. Now stitch on the waistband from the inside, fold over along the fold line, and top-stitch to the right side close to the edge. Beginning 6 cm (2½") from the center front, stitch across the waistband to make 2 casings of equal width. Stitch and turn the straps and stitch on with the straight ends at the

Enlarge the pattern pieces for the bag from the measurements on the diagram. Numbers are centimeters; inch equivalents are given.

The sleeping bag fits snugly at the waist. It is zipped up the front and the straps cross at the back.

front; the slanted ends crossed over, are at the back. Top-stitch close the upper edge of the waistband, catching in the straps. Cut the elastic in 2 lengths and draw through the casings; stitch across the ends.
Finally, turn in the seam allowance of the opening and stitch in the zipper.

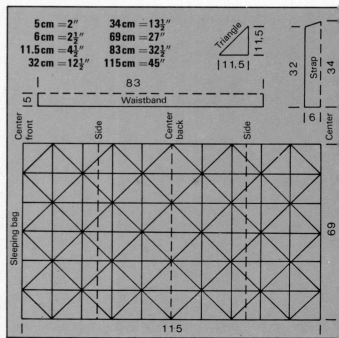

5 cm = 2"	34 cm = 13½"
6 cm = 2½"	69 cm = 27"
11.5 cm = 4½"	83 cm = 32½"
32 cm = 12½"	115 cm = 45"

Triangle 11.5 11.5

Strap 32 34 6 Center

83 5 Waistband

Center front 5 | Side | Center back | Side | Center

Sleeping bag 69

115

Make it Bavarian

If you spend time in the country, you will love these styles. They are comfortable, casual, and classic enough to see you through the changing fads in fashion.

Style 1: (in sizes D and F) Be a pretty peasant in this gaily-printed cotton dress and crisp white apron. Green rickrack accentuates the seams of the front and back bodice, while small green buttons decorate the front opening. The wide skirt is gathered at the back and pleated at the front. The apron has a tuck trimmed with rickrack and long ties that wrap around to the front.

Style 1

Style 2

Style 3

Style 4: (in sizes C and E) Culottes are a stylish, yet practical part of any country wardrobe. This gabardine skirt is slightly flared and has additional width provided by the deep pleats in the center front and back. The zipper is in the center front seam and we've given you useful pockets at each side.

On the man's style there are two back pockets with buttoned flaps. ◄

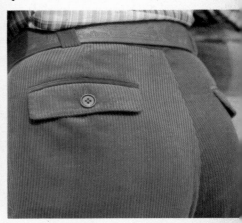

Style 2: (in sizes B and D) Knee breeches or knickerbockers are practical and comfortable for hiking and walking. Those illustrated are in corduroy and fasten at the front with a zipper. The pockets are top-stitched, and the legs are drawn in just below the knee with buckles.

Style 3: (in sizes M and O) Use a wider-ribbed cord for the man's breeches. Here, flapped pockets at the back are fastened with buttons, while the side pockets are open and double-stitched. Note the belt loops and the buckle fastening below the knee.

Style 4

The tabs for ► the buckles on both styles are top-stitched with decorative crosses. This adjustable knee band draws in the pant leg for a snug fit.

◄ On the woman's style, the back sports a pointed yoke which is both decorative and ensures a good fit. Top-stitch twice for a neat finish.

Flapped pocket with piping

This style of flapped pocket, finished with piping, is often incorporated into men's pants and jackets, so it is useful to know how it is worked. For clarity, we have used different fabrics for the pocket parts so that you can easily identify them and the various stages will be easy to understand. One thing you can be sure of is that your care and patience will be well rewarded with a professional finish.

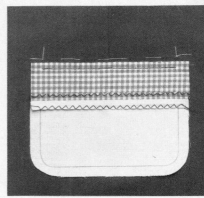

2 Stitch the dart, then press it. Stitch the lower strip of piping (with pocket lining attached) to the lower marked line, right sides facing and with seam allowances of 0.5 cm ($\frac{1}{4}$"). Stitch from one corner to the other exactly.

3 Pin the upper strip of piping to 0.5 cm ($\frac{1}{4}$") along the upper marked basting line with the raw edges facing downward. Then stitch the piping strip in place exactly from corner to corner.

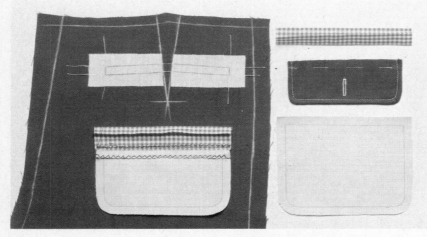

1 You will need the lower and upper pocket lining plus the pocket flap. You will find the patterns for these on the pattern sheet. Note that you can make the pocket linings from special lining fabric or taffeta, in a matching color. For the upper piping, cut a strip 16 cm ($6\frac{1}{4}$") long by 3 cm ($1\frac{1}{4}$") wide, then press it in half lengthwise. Cut the lower strip of piping 16 cm ($6\frac{1}{4}$") long and 5 cm (2") wide, then press back 1 cm ($\frac{3}{8}$") along one long side. Stitch the other long side to the lower pocket lining, right sides facing, with a seam allowance of 1 cm ($\frac{3}{8}$"). Depending on the thickness of the fabric, either press the seam open or downward. Finish the raw edges. Noting that the finished width of the piping is 0.5 cm ($\frac{1}{4}$"), mark the piping placement lines with basting. Reinforce the slit with strips of iron-on woven interfacing. Cut two strips each 9 cm ($3\frac{1}{2}$") long by 4 cm ($1\frac{1}{2}$") wide and iron them on either side of the dart to avoid excessive bulk. Interface the upper pocket flap with iron-on woven interfacing. Baste along line marked at top of flap. Stitch and turn flap (on thicker fabrics, use taffeta for under side). Top-stitch and work a buttonhole where marked.

4 Pin the flap, wrong side facing right side, to the upper pocket lining, then stitch together along the seam allowance. Note that the flap is slightly narrower than the width of the finished pocket to allow for the piping.

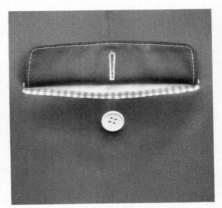

the inside and stitch to the piping. Secure the ends of the threads well. Check that the pocket linings lie flat on one another. It does not matter if the marked lines do not line up exactly. Finish the seam allowances all around.

5 Place the pocket flap (with the lining) over the upper piping strip, right sides facing. Pin together from the wrong side and baste over the pins with diagonal basting stitches. Then, working from the wrong side, stitch along the piping seam through all layers. For clarity, we have shown this stage from the right side.

8 Then turn the upper pocket lining to the wrong side and pin it together all around along the marked line. Finish the raw edges of the piping and pocket lining together.

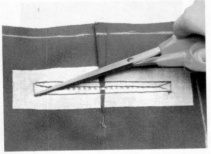

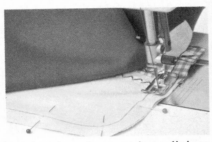

6 Cut garment fabric only from the wrong side, cutting exactly between the two lines of stitching. Then clip diagonally into the corners.

9 Stitch the pocket linings together all around, catching the small triangles created when cutting into the corners. Turn to

10 Finally, sew the button onto the pocket, taking care not to sew through to the pocket lining on the inside.

7 First turn the lower pocket lining to the wrong side. Fold the seam allowances created by cutting the slit up toward the piping. Pin the piping to show 0.5 cm ($\frac{1}{4}''$) and stitch down along the seamline from the right side.

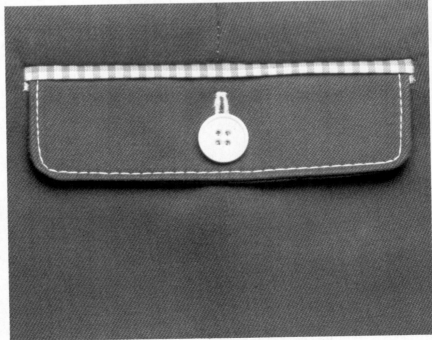

Here is the finished pocket, complete with flap and piping.

Style 1:
In sizes
D and F.

Style 3:
In sizes
B and D.

Style 2:
In sizes
C and E.

ur skirt parade gives you six skirt styles in a wide range of sizes, so there's sure to be one to suit ou. The emphasis is on a narrow silhouette which complements both feminine and sporty styles. ll of the skirts are simple to sew and are found on Pattern Sheet 72.

Illustrated
Sewing
72

Style 5:
In sizes
C and E.

Style 4:
In sizes
B and D.

Style 6:
In sizes
A and C.

Waistband pocket

This cleverly-designed detail has a double function. Not only is it a neat little flapped pocket, but it acts as a loop for the belt. Don't use too bulky a fabric; cotton and gabardine are best. Note that we have used a plain and a patterned fabric for clarity.

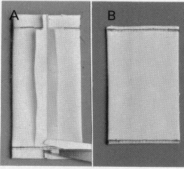

1 Cut out the pocket once on the fold with a seam allowance of 1 cm ($\frac{3}{8}$″) on all edges. Mark one crosswise seamline and the fold lines with basting. Stitch the center seam and press open the seam. Fold the pocket in half along the fold lines, then stitch the unmarked crosswise seamline, fastening off securely. Trim away the seam allowances of the center seam as shown in photograph A above so that the allowances are different widths and this part is not too bulky. Turn to the right side. Turn the seam allowances along the open side to the inside, then baste the edges together. Top-stitch both cross edges as shown in photograph B above.

2 Fold the pocket in half lengthwise, then baste and stitch both sides through all layers as shown in the photograph above.

3 Cut out the pocket flap in fabric with seam allowances of 1 cm ($\frac{3}{8}$″) on all edges. Cut it out in non-iron woven interfacing without seam allowances, then baste it onto the fabric. Mark the buttonhole with basting. Press in the seam allowances over the interfacing, beginning with the straight sides and then the points as shown.

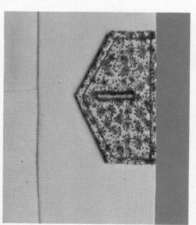

4 Fold the flap in half, wrong sides facing, and baste all around. Top-stitch the sides and point, close to the edge. Make a buttonhole where marked. Place the flap onto the waistband, straight edges matching, and stitch down, fastening the ends securely. The flap will look as shown in photograph 4.

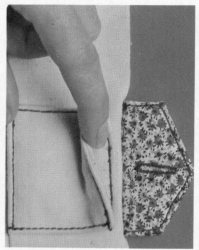

5 Pin the pocket under the flap, lining up the lower edge with the waistband seamline. Stitch along the bottom through all layers. Leave the sides unstitched for the belt. On the upper edge, stitch the back part of the pocket only to the waistband, as far as you can.

6 Finally, sew on the button. The photograph shows the completed pocket with the belt threaded behind it.

Style 1: This casual style in gabardine is cut quite straight. Two small pockets have been stitched onto the wide waistband, and these double as belt loops. Note the buttoned front opening.

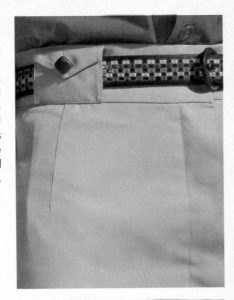

Style 4: Made up in a pretty cotton print, skirt number four is flared and gathered into the waist. Elastic is used for the waistband. The skirt buttons down the front and there are large patch pockets.

Style 2: A plaid fabric shows the details of this skirt to great advantage. It has a bias-cut hip yoke which comes to a point at the front and back. The side pockets have diagonal openings and there is a deep pleat down the front.

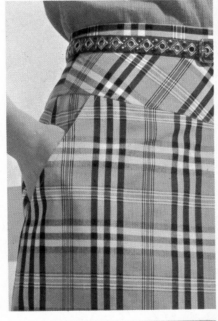

Style 5: Use crisp white for this sporty straight skirt — a jeans-type fabric would be best. The hip yoke at the back, the patch pockets, and the seams are top-stitched, jeans-style. There is a zipper in the front, and diagonal pocket openings at the sides. Slits at the side of the skirt aid movement.

Style 3: Here we have a wrap-around style. It's cut straight and is slightly gathered onto the waistband. It wraps over at the back and the ties button onto the waistband at the front. Two deep patch pockets are top-stitched onto the front.

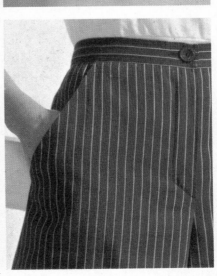

Style 6: These culottes are best worn by the tall and slim. The use of vertical stripes will flatter these features even more. It's cut quite straight and there is a front zipper. The waistband is secured with a button.

To make in sailcloth or heavy cotton

A bevy of bags for the beach

These three bright bags have been specially designed for use on the beach — they'll be indispensable for your summer days in the sun. Style 1 is spacious enough to hold a beachrobe and towel. Style 2 has a flap and holds smaller, more intimate items, and Style 3 is lined with plastic to hold your wet swimsuit. All the seams are trimmed with contrasting piping.

Style 1

Materials Required:
Sailcloth: 1.7 m (1⅞ yds), 90 cm (36") wide. Bias binding for piping: 3.2 m (3½ yds). Thread.

Cutting out: Add 1 cm (⅜") seam allowances on all edges. Cut out the side piece and side pocket once. Cut all other pieces twice. Cut two strips for the straps measuring 1.3 m (1½ yds) long by 6 cm (2½") wide plus a 1 cm (⅜") seam allowance all around.

Sewing: Stitch the facing to the upper edges of the bag, right sides together, as far as point **a**. Clip into the seam allowance at **a**, turn, and then top-stitch edge.

Patch pockets: Turn under the seam allowance, top and bottom, and attach piping to these edges. Stitch each pocket in place along side and bottom edges, then stitch down the center of the pocket.

Straps: Turn under the seam allowance and top-stitch each strap. Stitch the straps to the front and back pieces.

Side pockets: Turn under seam allowance at the top and attach piping. Turn in the remaining edges, pin to side, and stitch in place. Stitch facings to the upper parts of the sides, right sides facing, as far as point **a**.

Clip into the seam allowance at **a**, turn, and top-stitch.

Turn in the seam allowances around remaining edges of bag. Pin edges together and top-stitch up to point marked **a**, inserting piping into each seam line as you do so.

Style 2

Materials Required:
Sailcloth: 0.3 m (⅜ yd), 90 cm (36") wide. Bias binding for piping: 3.2 m (3½ yds). Thread. Press stud. Stud punch.

Cutting out: Add 1 cm (⅜") seam allowance. Cut out all the pattern pieces.

Sewing: The flap of the bag is cut in one with the back. With right sides facing and inserting piping into the seamline to 3 cm (1¼") above point **b**, stitch the facing to the flap to point **b**. Clip into the seam allowance at point **b**, turn, and top-stitch. Turn in the lower edge of the facing and stitch to the bag. Turn under the top edge of the front along the fold line and top-stitch 0.75 cm (¼") from the edge and again 2.5 cm (1") from the first stitching line. Stitch the completed front and back together, right sides facing, inserting piping into the seam along the bottom edge to just above the curve. Turn and top-stitch. Apply a press stud with a stud punch or a pair of pliers.

Style 3

Materials Required:
Sailcloth: 0.65 m (¾ yd), 90 cm (36") wide. Vinyl or PVC: 0.5 m (½ yd), 120 cm (48") wide. Bias binding for piping: 2.5 m (2¾ yds). Zipper. Thread.

Cutting out: Add 1 cm (⅜") seam allowance to all edges. Cut out the pattern for the bag twice from fabric and twice from vinyl or PVC. For the sides, cut two strips from fabric and two from vinyl or PVC, each 59.5 cm (23½") long by 5 cm (2") wide plus a 1 cm (⅜") seam allowance.

Sewing: Stitch the fabric and plastic as one piece when assembling the bag. Pin the side pieces together, right sides facing, and then stitch the strips into a circle. Turn in the seam allowances of the front and side. Stitch together all around, inserting piping into the seam as you do so. Repeat for the back and other edge of the side, but leave the zipper slit open. Insert the zipper neatly to finish.

Style 1: There is plenty of room inside and practical easy-access outside pockets.

Style 2: This small bag will hold your valuables and cosmetics neatly and safely.

Style 3: This version is lined with plastic to hold wet swimwear and sun tan oil.

Draw a grid on brown paper or tracing paper so that each square equals 3 cm (1¼"). Transfer the lines of the pattern pieces onto the grid, marking on all letters and instructions as shown on the graph below. Cut out the pieces for a complete full-size pattern for three useful beach bags.

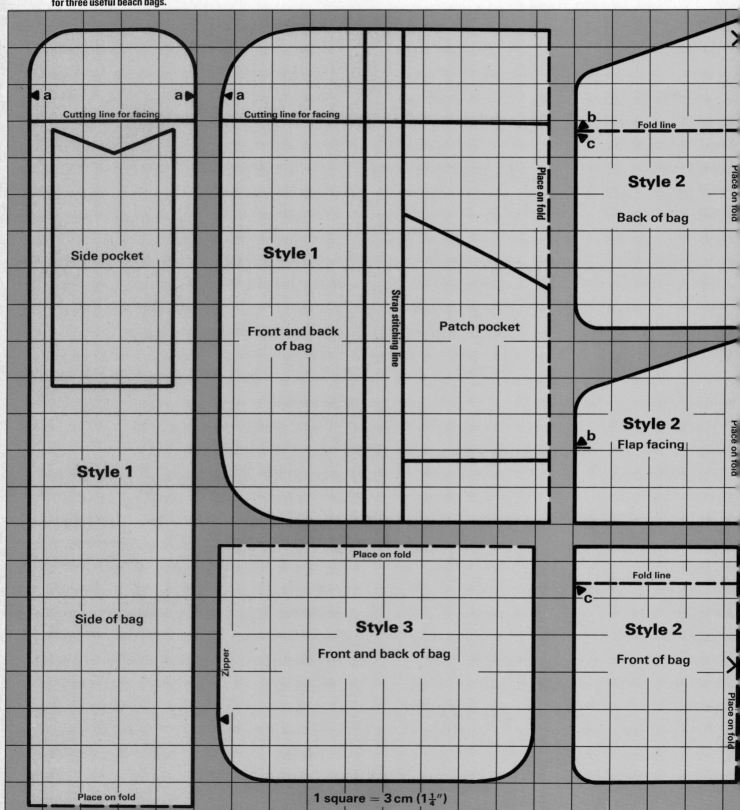

Cutting line for facing

a

Side pocket

Style 1

Cutting line for facing

a   a

Style 1

Front and back of bag

Strap stitching line

Patch pocket

Place on fold

b
c

Fold line

Style 2

Back of bag

Place on fold

Style 2

Flap facing

b

Side of bag

Zipper

Place on fold

Style 3

Front and back of bag

Fold line

c

Style 2

Front of bag

Place on fold

Place on fold

1 square = 3 cm (1¼")

easy to make from bright triangles

Sunscreen

You and your children will find many uses for the tents and screens you can make from these triangles.

Sunscreen or windscreen: Make this protective awning from two small and three large tent poles and six triangles.

Long tent: Make this from two tent poles and eight triangles. Ideal for beach or garden, it's big enough for all the family.

1 <u>Materials Required</u>: Canvas, sail-cloth, or tarpaulin: 140cm (55") wide, 3m (3¼ yds) for 3 triangles. Eyelet tool. Eyelets: 10mm (⅜") in diameter, 21 pairs per triangle. Heavy-duty thread. Nylon cord. Thick towelling to make 5cm (2") toggles for each pair of eyelets.

2 Draw the triangles on the fabric with a ruler and tailor's chalk. Each side should measure 150cm (59") in length.

3 Turn under the edges 2cm (¾") on all three sides, pinching them back firmly or pressing them down. Stitch with a thick needle and strong thread in zigzag stitch.

4 Mark and punch the holes for the corners. Then mark and punch the holes along the sides, regularly spaced

about 21cm (8¼") apart. Place a board under the fabric to protect the working surface.

5 Insert the eyelets: Place the cap in the groove of the punch and draw the fabric over.

6 Place the eyelet ring onto the shaft and the top part of the tool on top; hammer together.

7 Join the triangles with short toggles made from dowelling and nylon cord. Drill a hole through the center of each toggle.

8 This last photograph shows the cutting layout. 3m (3¼ yds) of fabric will give you three triangles with 2cm (¾") seam allowances. The half triangles can be seamed up the middle for a fourth triangle.

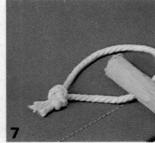

Making the triangles

The triangle is a basic shape which can be used to create tents, awnings, and screens of various shapes and sizes. We made triangles of brightly-colored plain canvas with equal sides and used them to make a number of clever designs to prove their versatility. There are many fabrics available for making up tents and awnings, of which canvas, sailcloth, and tarpaulin are just a few. They come in many weights, widths, and colors, too, so your choice should be guided by the requirements of your design. Look around in large stores, shops that specialize in heavyweight fabrics, and ship's chandlers.

The triangles illustrated were made up in medium-weight fabric 140 cm (55") wide. Always choose a thread suitable for the weight and fiber of the fabric being used.

Follow the step-by-step photographs for making up and joining the triangles. The eyelets are inserted with a special tool or punch. For every triangle you will need 21 eyelets and a punch with a diameter of approximately 10 mm ($\frac{3}{8}$"). Join the triangles together with toggles made from dowelling and nylon cord. Drill holes in the center of the dowels, thread the cord through, and knot the ends together. Thread the loop through the two eyelets and slip the dowel through the loop. Experiment with the length of the cord so that the pieces are joined closely as shown in picture 7. To put up the tent, screen, or awning, you will also require tent poles, tent pegs, and guy ropes. These are all available from specialist shops and camping departments of stores.

Square tent: Use one tent pole and four triangles for this play tent. It's easy enough for the children to put up themselves.

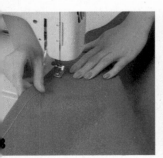

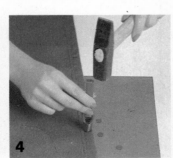

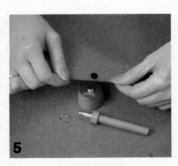

Cushion comfort

If you have any garden chairs made of cane or wood, you will need cushions to make them really comfortable. We show you here three different types of cushion which you can adapt to the shape of your chairs by drawing paper patterns of the seat and back. Make them in a strong fabric such as sailcloth.

Chairs 1 and 2: Straight-sided cushions made of 6 cm (2½″) thick foam rubber blocks.

Chairs 3 and 4: Shaped cushions filled with foam chips held in place with covered buttons.

Chair 5: Padded cover stitched in sections and stuffed with cushions.

If the chair is a reclining one add two or three more sections for extra length, or a removable extension with an open-ended zipper.

Cushions with straight edges

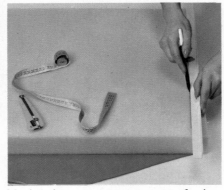

Mark the measurements of the chair seat onto the foam rubber block with a felt-tipped pen and ruler. Any curves should be marked with the help of a paper pattern which you have previously prepared.

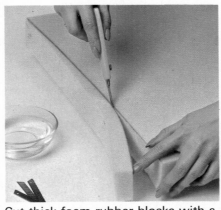

Cut thick foam rubber blocks with a sharp craft knife, holding the blade exactly perpendicular and straight. Thinner sheets of foam rubber (up to 3 cm (1″) thick) can also be cut with scissors which have been wetted.

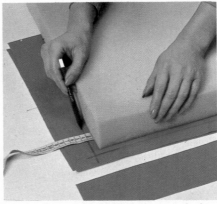

Mark the top and bottom of the cover with a 1 cm (⅜″) seam allowance and cut out. Cut out 3 side

strips to fit the thickness of the foam rubber plus 1 cm (⅜″) seam allowance. Divide the back strip in two (for zipper); cut out with seam allowance. Stitch in zipper.

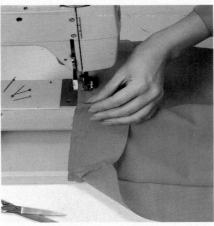

Join the 4 gusset pieces into a circle and stitch to both top and bottom, right sides facing. Leave the zipper open and turn to right side.

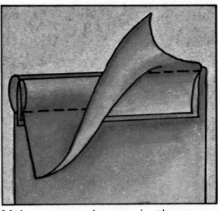

Make a second seam in the same way as a French seam all around the top and bottom, stitching close to the edges as shown. This makes the straight edges crisp.

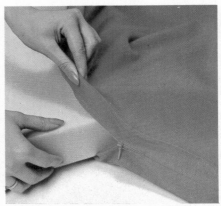

Push the foam rubber block into the fabric cover, fitting the edges along the seams.

Shaped cushions with buttons

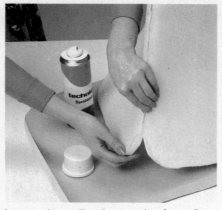

Materials Required: Foam rubber chips, sheets of foam rubber 1 cm ($\frac{3}{8}$″) thick. Spray adhesive. Covering fabric. Upholstery buttons.

Leave the adhesive to dry for a few minutes before proceeding. The adhesive-covered edges of the foam sheets must now be placed exactly onto one another and pressed together firmly.

Insert a zipper if desired. Place the cushion into the cover. If you do not require a zipper, join the opening by hand. Sew on the covered buttons with doubled buttonhole thread, sewing through all thicknesses.

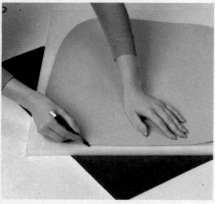

Padded cover

Cut out 2 pieces of fabric to the required size. Join along 1 long and 2 short sides, turn, and stitch across at about 20 cm (8″) intervals, stopping 1 cm ($\frac{3}{8}$″) from the edge of the open long side.

Make a pattern for the chair seat and draw around it onto the sheet of foam rubber. Cut out with scissors.
It is advisable to wet the scissors in between cuts.

Now stuff the foam cushion with the foam chips, but do not fill it too full.
The opening is then glued together in the same way as the other edges.

To stuff the sections, make small cushions: stitch 3 sides together, turn, and fill with foam chips. Sew the last seam from the right side.

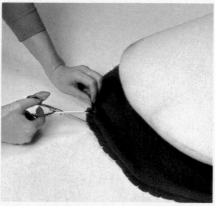

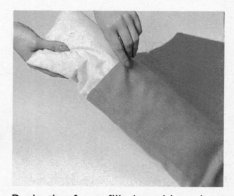

Now place the 2 sheets together and spray the cut edges all around with adhesive. Leave an opening of about 15 cm–20 cm (6″–8″) on one side for filling with the foam rubber chips.

Cut out the cover from the fabric, using a paper pattern for the seat or the foam cushion as a guide. Add 1 cm ($\frac{3}{8}$″) all around for seam allowance. Stitch the cover together, right sides facing and leaving a 20 cm (8″) opening. Snip into the seam allowance at frequent intervals all around.

Push the foam-filled cushions into the sections of the cover. Turn in the seam allowance along the open side and stitch close to the edge. Finally, top-stitch the other 3 sides close to the edge, taking care not to catch in the cushions.

Padded towelling beach mat

Sunspot

Relax in comfort on our wonderfully soft beach mat. We have made it striped on one side, plain on the other, but you can, of course, use the same fabric on both sides. It rolls up easily into a very small space and it can be washed in the washing machine.

Size: The finished beach mat is 85 cm (33½″) wide and 180 cm (70″) long.

Materials Required:
Striped towelling: 1.85 m (2 yds), 90 cm (36″) wide. Plain towelling: 1.85 m (2 yds), 90 cm (36″) wide. Machine-washable batting or wadding: 1.80 m (2 yds), 90 cm (36″) wide.

Making the mat
Cut the batting or wadding to measure the size of the mat without the seam allowance [i.e. 85 cm (33½″) x 180 cm (70″)]. Baste onto the wrong side of the plain fabric, leaving a 2.5 cm (1″) border all around. Divide the mat into 4 equal parts lengthwise; mark divisions with basting thread. Stitch the divisions. Stitch the striped fabric to the plain fabric, right sides facing, with a 2.5 cm (1″) seam allowance, leaving about 30 cm (11¾″) open on one short side for turning. Turn through to the right side and sew up the opening by hand.

Now divide the mat into 10 sections widthwise with basting thread. Stitch along the marked divisions. The plain side is thus divided up into squares, whereas the striped side has only widthwise seams. In this way, the batting or wadding is held firmly and will not bunch up.

Go backless for a super tan

This little top made up in a pretty printed cotton is meant for those really hot summer days. Worn with jeans or cotton skirts, it suits those without too much bust.

This summer top guarantees that you stay cool and expose a maximum of back to the sun. You can make it with or without the decorative frill. The straps tie at the back of the neck, and thin bands at the sides cross at the back and tie at the front.

Size: This teenage top is for girls with a bust measurement of approximately 80 cm (31½″).

Materials Required:
Fabric: 1.2 m (1⅜ yds), 90 cm (36″) wide. Thread.

Cutting out

Cut out the front twice. For straps, cut two strips measuring 65 cm (25⅝″) long and for waist bands two strips measuring 1.1 m (1¼ yds) long. Cut all strips 4 cm (1½″) wide plus seam allowances. For frills, cut bias strips measuring 8 cm (3″) wide and stitch together for a finished length of 2.5 m (2¾ yds) plus seam allowances.

Sewing the top

The top is double but the two parts are stitched separately and then joined together. Stitch darts. Fold the straps and bands in half lengthwise, right sides together, and stitch one short side and the long side. Turn with the aid of a pencil. For the frills, having stitched the bias strips together for the correct length, fold them in half lengthwise, right sides facing. Turn under the seam allowances on the narrow ends and sew closed by hand. Gather strip along open long side to measure 1 m (1⅛ yd) in length and then baste to top and sides of one of the fronts, right sides facing and the fold of the frill towards the garment. Baste the straps and bands in place also. Pin the second front in place, right sides facing, and stitch all around leaving a small opening for turning. Turn to right side, .close opening by hand, and top-stitch all around to finish.

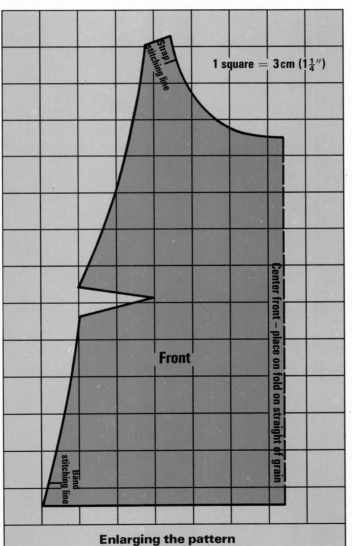

1 square = 3 cm (1¼″)

Strap stitching line

Front

Center front – place on fold on straight of grain

Band stitching line

Enlarging the pattern

Draw a grid of 3 cm (1¼″) squares onto brown paper or tracing paper. Then transfer the lines of the pattern from the graph above onto the grid, mark in all instructions, and cut out a full-sized pattern.

Quick and easy summer hats

Come rain or shine

Fashions in hats change as often as fashion itself, but this simple shape and style is always popular. You may decide to make it as a sun hat, but even if the weather turns rainy it will still look chic. It's easily made in an evening — and cheap, too!

Style 1: Use scraps of brightly colored cotton to make this gay little hat.

Style 2: Use a variety of flowered fabrics, all of which have the same background color – in this case black. The effect is original.

Style 3: This simple denim style can be worn everywhere – even on the beach. It is light enough to be folded up and packed into a bag in case of wind or rain, or in a suitcase for your summer travels.

◄ Style 4: Here is a very pretty idea. Make the basic hat from plain cotton and trim the brim with brightly colored ribbons attached with a single line of top-stitching. Thread colors contrast with the ribbons.

Size: The pattern is made for a head size of 58 cm (23"). Measure the circumference of your head and alter the pattern slightly if necessary.

Cutting out: Cut out the crown piece ten times. Place brim on fold line of double fabric and cut out twice, or four times for a double brim. Add 0.5 cm ($\frac{1}{4}$") seam allowance on all edges.

Sewing: Stitch five crown pieces together, stitching from the lower edge to the point. Press seams open and top-stitch close to seamline. Repeat to make another crown. Place crowns together, wrong sides facing; pin around lower edges. Stitch together around lower edge.

Stitch side seams of brim and press open. For single brim, turn under outer seam allowance and top-stitch. For double brim, stitch two brims together, right sides facing. Turn to right side and press edge; baste inner edges together. Stitch brim to crowns, right sides facing. Press allowances up into brim after clipping and then top-stitch along seam.

Style 1: Fabric: Brightly-colored scraps. Top-stitch brim close to outer edge and seven times more at regular intervals.

Style 2: Fabric: Various flowered prints. Top-stitch brim close to outer edge.

Style 3: Fabric: Denim. Top-stitch brim close to edge, then nine times more at regular intervals.

Style 4: Fabric: Plain cotton and 1 m (1$\frac{1}{8}$ yd) each of ribbon in four colors. Top-stitch to brim at regular intervals.

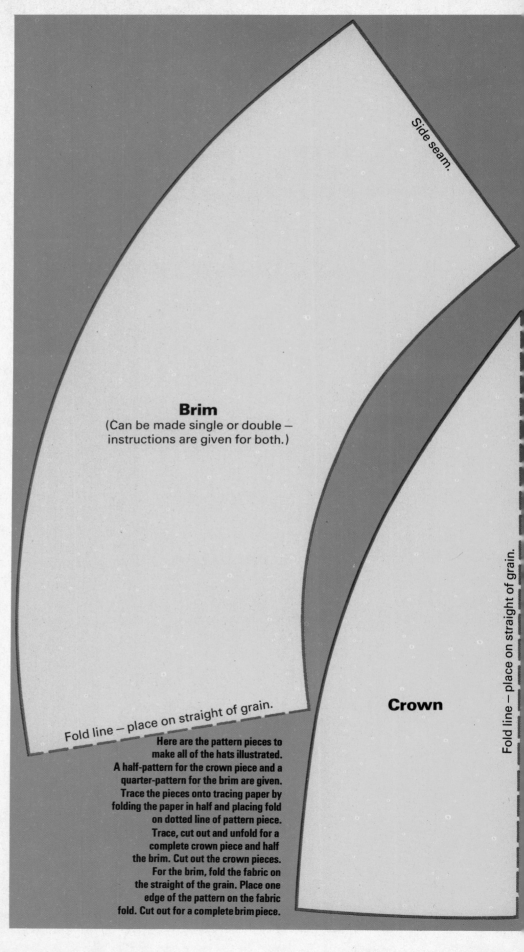

Side seam.

Brim
(Can be made single or double — instructions are given for both.)

Fold line — place on straight of grain.

Crown

Fold line — place on straight of grain.

Here are the pattern pieces to make all of the hats illustrated. A half-pattern for the crown piece and a quarter-pattern for the brim are given. Trace the pieces onto tracing paper by folding the paper in half and placing fold on dotted line of pattern piece. Trace, cut out and unfold for a complete crown piece and half the brim. Cut out the crown pieces. For the brim, fold the fabric on the straight of the grain. Place one edge of the pattern on the fabric fold. Cut out for a complete brim piece.

Put your best foot forward

Step out in style this summer in a pair of flower-embroidered and laced espadrilles — the perfect light-hearted accessory for jeans and cotton skirts.

Materials Required:

A pair of plain canvas espadrilles (see photograph above). Scraps of stranded cotton in bright colors. Cotton tape: 5 m ($5\frac{1}{2}$ yds), 1 cm ($\frac{3}{8}$") wide.

Decorating the shoes

Using undivided stranded cotton and a strong, pointed needle, embroider the flowers in lazy daisy stitch in various colors. Work them large or small, singly or in groups. The flowers can be worked in a random pattern with large and small flowers to cover up worn places in an old pair of espadrilles. In the larger flowers, fill in the centers in satin stitch and the petals with an extra daisy stitch. The edge of the blue shoe has been embroidered in blanket stitch in a contrasting color. To secure the laces, cut 5 lengths of tape per shoe, each 4 cm ($1\frac{3}{4}$") long. Fold in half and sew the loops to the inside of the shoes so that 1 cm ($\frac{3}{8}$") protrudes. Position one loop at the center front and two at equal distances on each side. Cut lengths of tape measuring 2.30 m ($2\frac{1}{2}$ yds) for the laces and thread them through the loops so that the ends are at the back. Lace the shoes by crossing the tapes over at back and front and tying into a bow.

2267

Embroidery

T-shirts for summer
Be a sport!

Are you a racing fan or a golf addict? Or do you prefer tennis and swimming? Whatever your favorite sport, there will be a motif here to suit you.

The T-shirts are embroidered with two strands of stranded cotton in stem stitch for the outlines and satin stitch for the filled-in areas. The colors used for the motifs illustrated are blue, grey, green, yellow, rust, red, pink, brown, and turquoise, but you could choose quite different colors if you prefer. As only small amounts of embroidery cotton are required, you can use up all of your oddments.

Trace the chosen motif and transfer it to your T-shirt with dressmaker's carbon paper. Baste a piece of organza onto the back to prevent the fabric from stretching as you embroider and mount it in a small embroidery frame.

The separate motifs are worked in the following colors:

Style 1 = blue, grey, green, yellow.
Style 2 = red, green, yellow, blue.
Style 3 = blue, yellow, red, grey.
Style 4 = red, blue, turquoise, yellow, grey.
Style 5 = grey, green, red, blue, pink.
Style 6 = red, green, yellow, grey, brown, pink, turquoise.
Style 7 = green, red, yellow, grey.
Style 8 = yellow, grey, red, turquoise.
Style 9 = red, green, blue, rust, pink, yellow.
Style 10 = blue, red, grey.

When the embroidery is complete, cut away the organza around the motif, and draw out the remaining threads with a pair of tweezers.

3 & 4

5 & 6

7

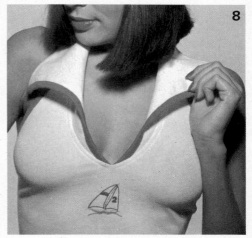

8

9

10

Sporting motifs

Choose your favorite sport and embroider an appropriate motif onto a plain T-shirt. Simple stitches are used for these light-hearted designs.

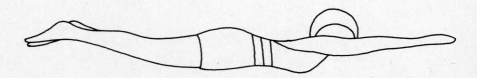

Bowling

Mitering a corner

Using our place mat as an example, we show you here how to miter a corner on a double hem.

1 First, mark the two hem fold lines with basting along the fabric grain. The inner basting line is the outer edge of the mat and lies 3 cm (1¼") from the outer drawn-through thread. The outer basting line lies 3 cm (1¼") further out, and 2 cm (¾") from the outside raw edge. Press along the basting.

2 Now mark the innermost corner formed by the basting threads with a pin and turn the fabric back at an exact diagonal through this corner point. Press down along the fold line.

3 Cut away the corner about 1 cm (⅜") in from the folded edge.

4 Turn in the hem twice and sew down close to the outer drawn-through thread. Slip-stitch the diagonal seam together at the corner, catching in only one thread of the hem at a time.

Setting the mood

For meals in the garden or on the patio, these place mats will fit the bill perfectly. The decorative border is quickly built up by drawing through lengths of pearl cotton in contrasting colors.

Size: 40 cm x 52 cm (15¾" x 20½").

Materials Required:
Rectangles of burlap or hessian measuring 54 cm x 66 cm (21¼" x 26") in red, orange, blue and green. Pearl cotton No. 5: 3 skeins each in red, orange, blue, and green. Sewing thread.

Making the mats
Draw out the threads around the edge of each rectangle for about 1 cm (⅜"). Cut pearl cotton into lengths double that of the edges, ie. 132 cm (52") and 108 cm (42½"). Measure in 9 cm (3⅝") from last thread at outer edge on one side and pull out left-hand end of 1 thread slightly until you can see where right-hand end comes out. Fold a length of pearl cotton in half. Divide

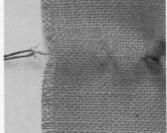

Knot one of the threads around the doubled pearl cotton and pull through the weave of the fabric.

left-hand end of woven thread and knot around the center of the doubled pearl cotton. Press knot flat with your fingers to enable it to slip through fabric more easily. Pull right-hand end of woven thread until it comes right out, drawing pearl cotton with it to replace it. Continue weaving pearl cotton threads from outside toward center of mat as follows: Weave 2 adjacent threads, skip 2 fabric threads, weave 1, skip 2 fabric threads, weave 2, skip 2 fabric threads, weave 1, skip 1 fabric thread, weave 2, skip 3 fabric threads, weave 1. On each place mat, draw through the colors of the other 3 mats in any attractive color sequence. Repeat the same color and weaving sequence on the other 3 sides. Press the mats so that the pearl cotton threads do not pucker the fabric. Then trim off the fabric to 8 cm (3¼") from the outer pearl cotton threads. Hem the mats, mitering the corners as shown in the How-to photographs opposite.

Fruit and vegetables to appliqué
Apply yourself

These appliqué motifs are a real feast for the eyes! Cut from scraps of cotton, they are outlined in blanket stitch with details in satin and stem stitch and French knots.

Size: The place mat illustrated measures 50 cm x 35 cm ($19\frac{5}{8}$" x $13\frac{3}{4}$").

Materials Required: (for 2 place mats) Linen: 1.20 m ($1\frac{3}{8}$ yds), 90 cm (36") wide. Piping: 3 m ($3\frac{1}{4}$ yds). Cotton remnants. Oddments of stranded cotton. Fine iron-on interfacing.

Making the mats

All the fruit on these two pages is shown actual size. Trace the separate pieces onto tracing paper and transfer them onto the adhesive side of the interfacing with dressmaker's carbon paper. Cut them out and iron them onto the relevant fabric remnants. Where two shapes overlap, add 0.5 cm ($\frac{1}{4}$") seam allowance on the underlap. Where two shapes of the same fabric meet, cut out the two parts together rather than separately and embroider the separating lines in stem stitch in the same color as on the pineapple leaves or carrots. Use 3 strands of cotton for the embroidery. The appliqué edging is worked in blanket stitch. All lines on the motifs are in stem stitch; smaller areas such as stems, shoots, or grass in satin stitch. The dots on the orange and the onion are French knots. To finish the mats, turn hem to right side, mitering the corners. Turn in seam allowance and stitch, catching in the piping.

Embroider this satin stitch picture and frame it as a colorful reminder of last summer or as a foretaste of the next!

Memories are made

Size: The finished picture is 37 cm (14½") wide and 25 cm (10") high.

Materials Required:
Even-weave linen or linen mixture with about 133 threads to 10 cm (34 threads to 1"): Piece measuring 52 cm x 40 cm (20½" x 16"). Stranded cotton in the following colors and quantities: 1 skein each of pale green, mid green, dark green, grey, dark grey, yellow, pale orange, orange, red, brown, salmon, pale blue, white, and black; 2 skeins each of dark blue, medium blue, sky blue. Dressmaker's carbon paper. Embroidery frame.

Working the picture

The design is given as a full-size pattern to trace. Transfer centrally onto the fabric with dressmaker's carbon paper along straight of grain. Using an embroidery frame, embroider all areas in satin stitch with 3 strands of the cotton, always inserting the needle between 2 fabric threads. No fabric should be visible between the embroidered areas, i.e., insert needle through same hole as stitch of adjacent area. Follow the photograph for the direction of the stitches and the colors of the different areas. The thin lines on the pattern indicate area boundaries.
Outlines such as the faces are worked in back stitch. If the fabric has distorted slightly during stitching, stretch it right side down onto a soft surface and cover with a damp cloth. Stretch the picture over hardboard and frame the picture as desired.

Salad days

Our picnic case holds everything that you will need for a carefree "al fresco" meal.

An ordinary fiber-board suitcase can be transformed into a smart picnic case. It is sturdy, and roomy enough to accommodate your knives and forks, thermos, plates, and glasses as well as the food. It is also well-insulated and has a compartment to hold ice packs which will keep the food cool.

Size: The inside measurements of the case illustrated are 25 cm x 42 cm (10" x 16½"), 11 cm (4½") deep, with a 3.5 cm (1½") deep lid. This is large enough for a picnic for three people. The same technique can be used for a picnic case of any size.

Materials Required: Paint in a can or aerosol. Vinyl-coated fabric: 1.50 m (1⅝ yds), 100 cm (39") wide. Cardboard to fit base, sides, and lid. Sheets of expanded polystyrene, 1 cm (⅜") thick to fit base, lid, and sides. Glue. About 70 upholsterers' tacks or studs. 2 punch-in press studs or snaps. Craft knife. Tenon saw. Piece of plywood, 6 mm (¼") thick, to fit inside the case.

moving the can while spray-painting, first from top to bottom, then from left to right. Leave the paint to dry well between coats.

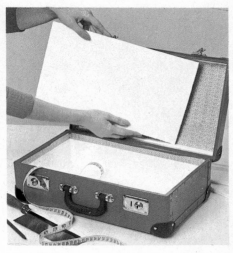

2 The case is lined with polystyrene to insulate it. Measure the base, lid, and sides, and cut out pieces to fit with a tenon saw, making the sides shorter than the case sides. Move the saw with a pulling motion only to avoid cracking the polystyrene. First glue the side strips lightly and insert into the case. Then fit the lid and base sheets in tightly. Now measure the base and sides again and draw the areas onto the cardboard, extending the sides out from the base. Cut out with a craft knife against a metal ruler. All around the base, score lightly along the lines to enable you to bend up the sides (see the cardboard in the photograph below). Draw and cut out the lid in the same way.

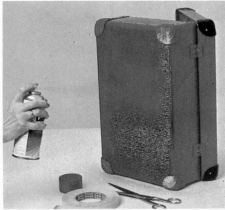

1 The case is painted first, either with a brush or a spray. Cover the handle, locks, and corners with masking tape before you begin. Paint the case several times (at least three times if using spray paint). Keep

3 Then place both base and lid patterns onto the wrong side of the vinyl-coated fabric and cut out with a 2 cm (¾") seam allowance all

around. At the corners, either snip into the fabric or cut across diagonally. Then coat the outer edges of the cardboard base and lid with glue (the sides are glued later). Also apply glue to the same areas on the wrong side of the fabric. Leave to dry slightly for about 10–15 minutes, then place the surfaces together precisely. Press together well, making sure that no wrinkles form.

Now glue the sides in the same way, making sure that no wrinkles form. Then, the 2 cm ($\frac{3}{4}$") wide allowances are glued down. Here also, both the fabric and the edge of the paper are covered with glue.

Finally, fold the sides into a box shape.

4 The fabric-lined box shape should fit tightly into the case covering the polystyrene strips. The same applies to the lid with its narrower sides. Push them firmly into place.

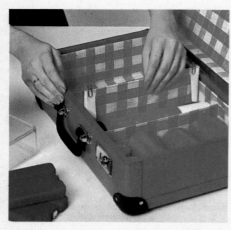

5 The case is then divided into three sections: for glasses, for a thermos flask, and for the food compartment. Cut out two pieces of cardboard to fit and glue fabric onto both sides, leaving 2 cm ($\frac{3}{4}$") over at each end.

Slot the divisions into the case, turning the ends back with paper clips. Then apply glue to these ends and to adjacent sides of the case, and glue together.

6 We made a tray from the sheet of plywood, which also serves as a dividing lid during transport. At the narrow ends, saw out gripholes with a tenon saw and sand all edges. The surfaces can be covered in vinyl-coated fabric or adhesive plastic in a matching color.

Plates and knives and forks are held in two pockets in the lid, each measuring 21 cm x 18 cm (8$\frac{1}{4}$" x 7"). Make yours to fit your own case.

7 Plate pocket: Draw the required shape onto cardboard, then cut out and round off the two upper corners. Glue the cardboard onto the wrong side of a large piece of fabric. At each side, draw an equal-sided triangle on the fabric. The upper edge should be 8 cm (3") long; the triangle points downwards.

Cut out the pocket, adding 2 cm ($\frac{3}{4}$") at the sides and bottom. Cut out the entire pocket once more in fabric and glue to the first pocket shape. The

added allowances are turned in an glued to the lid of the case.

Then glue 2 strips of fabric togethe and cut out a tab measuring 11 cm 6 cm (4$\frac{1}{2}$" x 2$\frac{1}{2}$") and another piec measuring 4 cm x 6 cm (1$\frac{1}{2}$" x 2$\frac{1}{2}$" Round off the corners. Punch th halves of a press stud or snap int the two parts. Glue the tab to th inside of the pocket with an underla of 4 cm (1$\frac{1}{2}$"); glue the other pa onto the lid. The plates fit neatly int this pocket, which opens out a shown in the photograph.

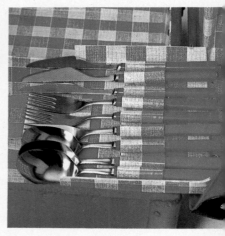

8 The knife and fork pocket is th same size as the plate pocke with rounded edges, but it has 3 cm (1$\frac{1}{4}$") walls on the sides and bottom Cut the shape in cardboard and glu fabric onto both sides. The bottom wall is glued onto the lid side. Mak the tab parts as for the plate compart ment. To hold the knives and forks i place, stitch a 4 cm (1$\frac{1}{2}$") wide stri of double fabric in loops onto anothe strip, then glue this to the inside o the pocket.

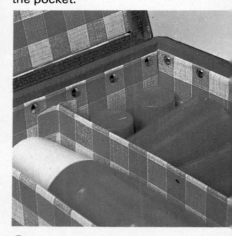

9 Fasten the base and lid insert onto the frame with the tacks o studs; if possible, fasten the two pockets to the lid in the same way.

Long skirts
with flowers

Fiesta fashions

If you like
unusual clothes
with great impact,
then why not
paint flowers
on a ruffled
peasant skirt
and shawl
with fabric
paints. The
motifs are
given as an
actual-size
pattern.

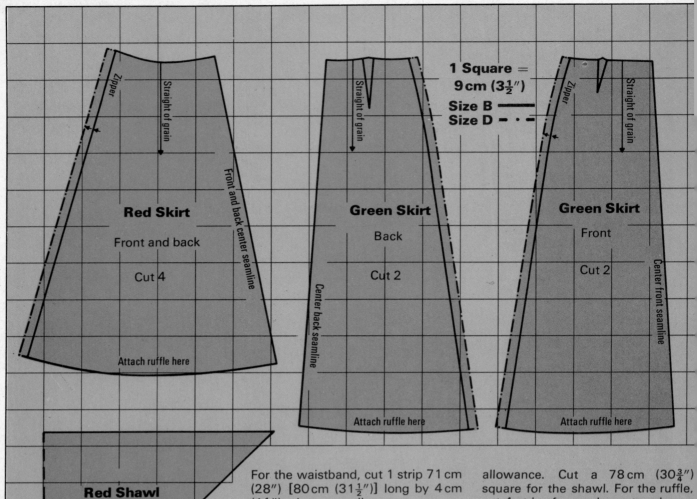

Red Skirt

Front and back

Cut 4

Zipper

Straight of grain

Front and back center seamline

Attach ruffle here

Green Skirt

Back

Cut 2

Straight of grain

Center back seamline

Attach ruffle here

1 Square = 9 cm (3½″)
Size B ———
Size D – · – ·

Green Skirt

Front

Cut 2

Zipper

Straight of grain

Center front seamline

Attach ruffle here

Red Shawl

Cut 1

Half-pattern line

Straight of grain

To enlarge the pattern, draw a grid of 9 cm (3½″) squares on tissue or tracing paper and transfer pattern outlines to new grid.

Sizes: B for 63.5 cm or 25″ waist, 90 cm or 35½″ hip and D for 72.5 cm or 28½″ waist, 98 cm or 38½″ hip. Measurements for larger size are in square brackets.

RED SKIRT

Materials Required: Cotton: 6 m (6½ yds) [6.1 m (6⅔ yds)], 90 cm (36″) wide. Waistband interfacing: 2 cm (¾″) wide to fit waist. Hooks and eyes. Zipper. Thread.

Cutting out: Add a 2 cm (¾″) seam allowance to all pieces. For ruffle, cut 5 straight strips from selvage to selvage, each 32 cm (12⅝″) wide.

For the waistband, cut 1 strip 71 cm (28″) [80 cm (31½″)] long by 4 cm (1½″), plus seam allowance.

Sewing: Stitch the ruffle strips in 1 long strip, ready for painting, but do not make a circle. Transfer motifs with dressmaker's carbon. Paint 8 motifs along the ruffle and a stripe at the hem fold line. Join the skirt pieces at the center front and side seams and paint a stripe along the lower edge. Paint a stripe around the shawl edges and a motif at the center back. Let dry. Then join the center back skirt seam. Join the ruffle to form a circle. Turn up the hem, gather the ruffle and stitch to the skirt. Sew in the zipper and gather the skirt to fit the waist measurement. Make a waistband with a 3 cm (1¼″) overlap. Sew on hooks and eyes. Shawl: turn under the raw edges twice and stitch.

GREEN SKIRT

Materials Required: Cotton: 3.70 m (4 yds) [3.80 (4⅛ yds)], 90 cm (36″) wide. Waistband interfacing: 3 cm (1¼″) wide to fit waist. Hooks and eyes. Zipper. Thread.

Cutting out: Add a 2 cm (¾″) seam allowance. Cut a 78 cm (30¾″) square for the shawl. For the ruffle, cut 4 strips from selvage to selvage, each 19 cm (7½″) wide. For the waistband, cut a strip 71 cm (28″) [80 cm (31½″)] long and 6 cm (2½″) wide, plus seam allowances.

Sewing: Stitch the darts in the skirt back and front pieces. Join the center seams and one side seam. Transfer motifs with dressmaker's carbon. Paint 2 double rows of stripes 1 cm (⅜″) and 20 cm (8″) from the lower edge. Paint 3 motifs each on the front and back between these stripes. On the shawl, paint 2 stripes all around edges and a motif in one corner. Let dry. Join the other side seam of the skirt. Join the ruffle strips into a circle. On one long side, turn under a 3 cm (1¼″) wide hem; on the other side, finish raw edge with zigzag stitch, then make a small head by turning under a 1.5 cm (⅝″) seam allowance. Gather ruffle. Stitch to skirt. Make waistband with a 3 cm (1¼″) overlap and stitch to the skirt. Sew on hooks and eyes. To make the shawl, fold in half, turn in the raw edges, and top-stitch all around.

Painting on cotton fabric

The flowers on the peasant skirts are painted onto the cotton with fabric paints. For the red and white flowers, you need carmine, white, pale green, dark green, and yellow. For the blue and red flowers, you need blue, carmine, green, white, and black. Fabric colors can normally be fixed by ironing on the reverse side of the fabric.

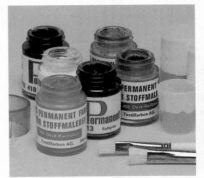

1 Materials Required: permanent fabric paints, 2 bristle paint brushes, paper cups for mixing, masking tape.

2 Stick tape along the fabric edges to make the stripes straight. Paint slightly over the tape, then peel it off.

3 Red/white flowers: Trace and transfer the motifs. Paint in white and pale green, covering the transfer lines neatly.

4 For the shading, dip the brush into the paint once, draw a curve, and smooth the paint outwards from it gradually.

5 For the shading on the leaves, lightly apply a little dark green. Leave to dry well and fix by ironing on the wrong side.

6 Blue/red flowers: Trace and transfer the motifs. Paint the flowers in basic colors of red and blue, the leaves in green.

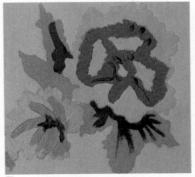

7 Now add the shading to the petals and leaves. Mix red, blue, and green with a little black to produce darker areas.

8 Finally, paint in the highlights by mixing white with the other colors. Leave to dry and fix by ironing on the wrong side.

Flowers for
Red Skirt

Flower painting on fabric

Use special fabric paints to decorate the edge of a long skirt with colorful blooms. Paint a shawl, too, to complete the outfit.

Flowers for
Green Skirt

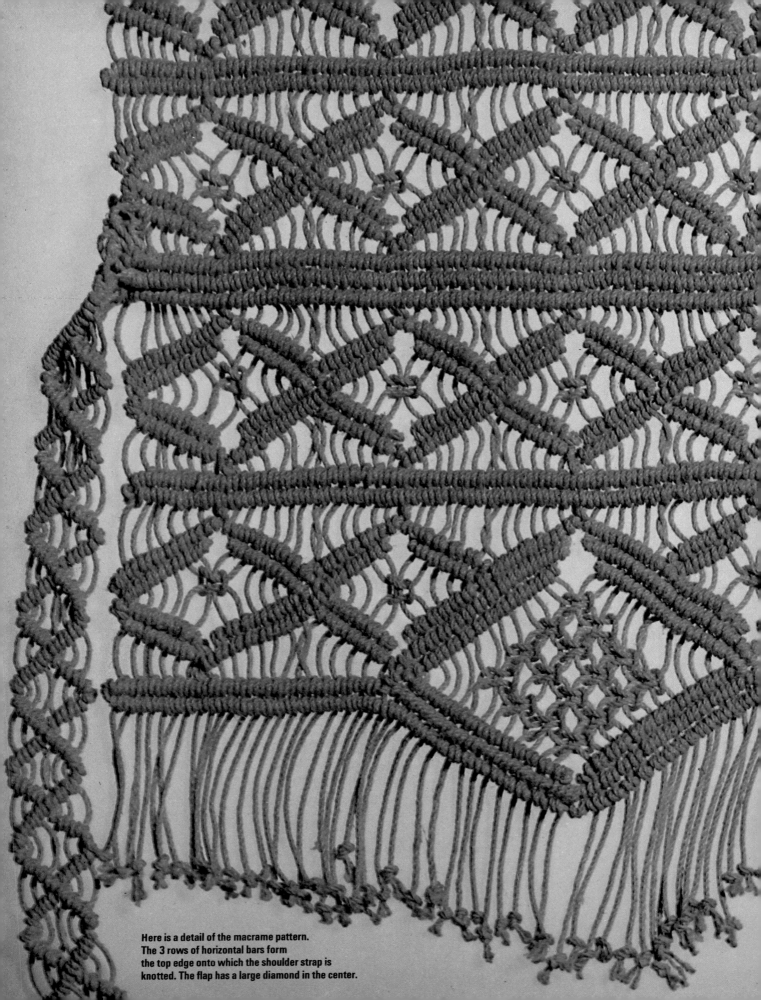

Here is a detail of the macrame pattern.
The 3 rows of horizontal bars form
the top edge onto which the shoulder strap is
knotted. The flap has a large diamond in the center.

Shoulder bag in macrame

Lacy diamonds in twine

Although there are relatively few macrame knots, by combining them in a variety of ways, an abundance of patterns can be created. This shoulder bag is made in bars and square knots, using parcel string.

Size: 29 cm (11¾") square.
Materials Required:
280 m (307 yds) parcel string. Mounting board.
Shoulder Strap: Cut 8 lengths of string 3 m (3¼ yds) in length. Work from the center out, knotting the diamond pattern in diagonal bars. When the strap measures 45 cm (17¾"), work the other half.
Bag: Cut 34 lengths of string 6.5 m (7⅛ yds) each and a mounting strand 14 m (15¼ yds). Make a simple knot at the center of the mounting strand and pin it to the base. Double the 34 strands of string and mount 17 strands onto the mounting strand to the right of the knot and 17 to the left. Work 1 horizontal bar, then work each of the 5 diamonds from the center out, working each diamond over 14 threads in diagonal bars. When the top half of the diamonds have been completed, make a square knot in the center of each one and then work the lower half. Work 2 horizontal bars over the mounting strand after each row of diamonds. After making 4 rows of diamonds, work 3 horizontal bars for the base, then 4 more rows of diamonds. For the top edge, work 3 horizontal bars. To begin the flap, work 1 row of diamonds and 2 rows of horizontal bars. In the next row, work the top half and square knots for the 4 outside diamonds, then in the center, work 3 diagonal bars to double the length to form a large diamond as shown. Fill the large diamond with square knots, then finish the small diamonds and work single diagonal bars for the large diamond. Finish with 2 horizontal bars. Trim strands and tie knots.
Finishing: Sew the sides together with string. Knot the strap to the top edge.

Square knot, Diagonal bar

Square knot

The square knot is made with two adjacent pairs of strands. The two outer threads are always placed alternately over and under the two center strands and each other.

Square knots can be worked singly, in horizontal rows, or in rows of alternating square knots. Alternating square knots are made by knotting together a pair of strands from each of two adjacent knots in the row above.

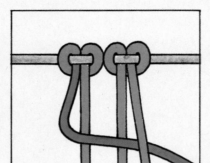

1 Place the left strand over the 2 center strands and under the right strand.

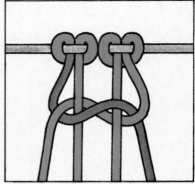

2 Place the right strand under the 2 center strands and over the left strand.

3 Place the left strand under the center strands, then the right strand over them as shown.

4 Make sure that the 2 center threads remain taut when the knot is pulled together.

Diagonal bar

A diagonal bar is made by knotting half hitches onto a strand slanting diagonally down to the left or right.

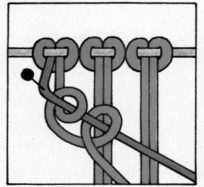

1 With each strand make a half hitch around the knot bearer. Pull knot tight.

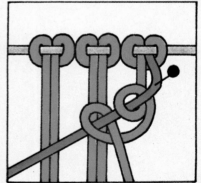

2 Work from right to left in the same way. Always hold the knot bearer taut.

Add a pretty finish to a flowered shawl with macrame fringe

fringe benefit

Materials Required:
Cotton fabric: 0.90 m (1 yd), 90 cm (36") wide. Cotton yarn: (shown actual-size below) 200 gm or 8 oz.

Macrame edging: Cut 4 mounting strands, each 2 m (2¼ yds) long. For the fringe, cut 316 strands each 80 cm (31½") long. Place the mounting strands in pairs, one below the other. Fold 300 of the fringe strands in half and knot onto the 2 upper mounting strands together. Work a horizontal bar of half hitches around the 2 lower strands together. Now work the top half of the diamonds from the center to the left edge. With first 10 strands, work diagonal bars down to the left, with next 10 strands, work 2 diagonal bars to the right, then repeat bars alternately to the left and right across (see photographs below). Make a square knot with the center

12 strands of each whole diamond, leaving the half diamond at the center of the edging. To complete the diamonds, begin at the center with 2 diagonal bars to the right and continue across as before.

Beginning at center, work other half in reverse.

For corner, make a right angle at center (see photograph). On each side, knot 5 new strands on last strand, 1 strand on each bar, and 1 strand on mounting strands. Connect the 2 sides with a semi-circle of bars as shown.

Make an ordinary knot at the base of each diamond to hold the bars together. Sew in the ends of the mounting cords.

Shawl: Cut an 86 cm (34") fabric square and press 1 cm (⅜") to the inside all around. Fold into a triangle, baste, and stitch close to the edge. Attach the macrame edging with backstitch.

Here is a detail of the edging. It shows a diamond made with diagonal bars of half hitches and a square knot worked with twelve strands in the center.

This photograph shows the way in which the corner is formed. Extra strands are mounted on and a semi-circle of bars connects the two sides.

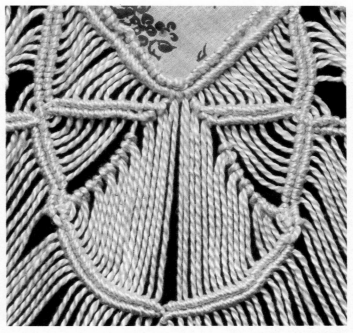

Attractive belts in macrame

Tie your outfit together

YELLOW BELT
Materials Required:
Cotton cording. Mounting board.
Basic Knots: Diagonal bars and square knots.

Making the belt
Cut 13 strands, each measuring 3 m (3¼ yds). Pin them to the board at their centers, so that you can work half the belt, then the other half. The left outer strand is the knot bearer. Work 1 row of diagonal bars, making a simple knot at the end of the row. In the second row, the next left outer strand is the knot bearer. Make a simple knot with this strand, then work a diagonal bar, making another simple knot at the end. Work the 3rd row with the next left outer strand in the same way.

Work a square knot with threads 3 to 6, counting from the left. Work 3 rows of diagonal bars from right to left. For each of these rows, the right outer strand is the knot bearer.

Repeat this pattern until you have 8 triangles. Knot the ends to secure them. Turn the work and knot the other half in the same way.

RED BELT
Materials Required:
Cotton cording. Mounting board.
Basic Knots: Diagonal bars and square knots.

Making the belt
Cut 12 strands, each measuring 3 m (3¼ yds). Pin them to the board at their centers, so that you can work one half, then the other.

Use strand 6, counting from the left, as the knot bearer. Skip strand 7 and work a diagonal bar with the remaining 5 strands. Make a simple knot at the en[d] Use strand 7 as the kn[ot] bearer for the diagonal b[ar] worked from right to left. The second row begins [at] the center again. For t[he] right diagonal bar, take t[he] strand from the first knot [of] the previous left diago[nal] bar, skip 1 strand, and kn[ot] with the remaining strands. For the left bar, t[he] skipped strand becomes t[he] knot bearer. Work a squa[re] knot with the center strands, then work 4 row[s] of diagonal bars. For ea[ch] row, use the outer left [and] right strand as the kn[ot] bearer and work 5 ha[lf] hitches from both sides [of] the center. In the seco[nd] row, cross the 2 cent[er] threads of the previous ro[w.] Work 2 more rows in t[he] same way. The next 4 row[s] are worked from the cent[er] out.

Make a square knot, fo[l]lowed by 2 rows of diago[nal] bars. Repeat this patte[rn] until 5½ diamonds hav[e] been worked. Turn the wo[rk] around and knot the oth[er] half in the same way. Kn[ot] the ends in groups [of] threads to secure them.

The diagram shows the belt patterns actual size. So that the position of the knots can be seen clearly, they are shown spaced wider apart than they will be when you knot the macrame cording.

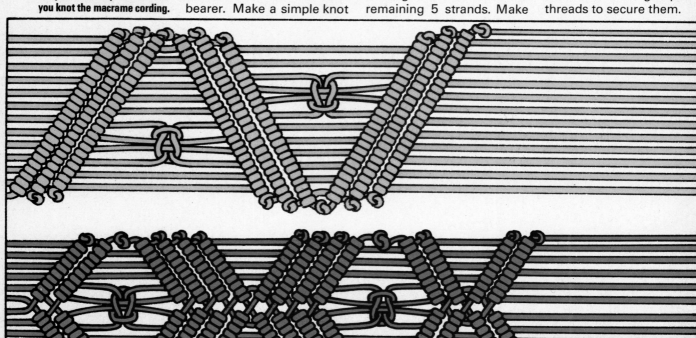

These two belts are worked in diagonal bars and square knots. Make them both to harmonize with a blouse or dress and wear them one above the other.

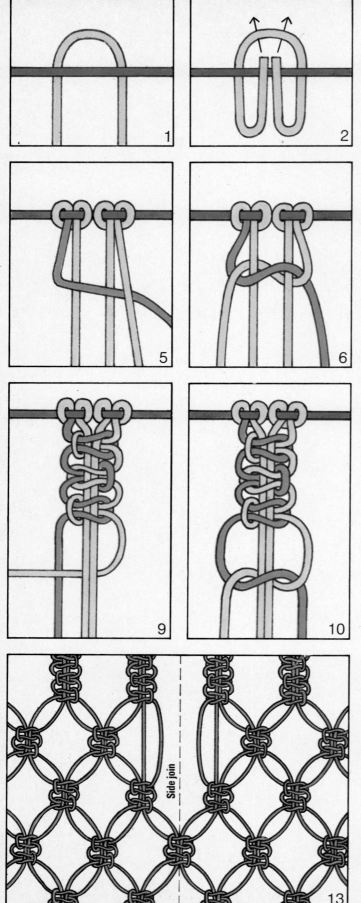

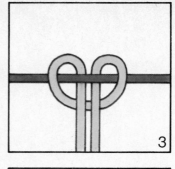

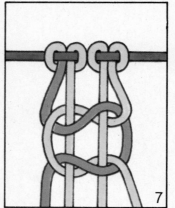

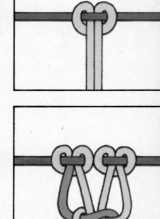

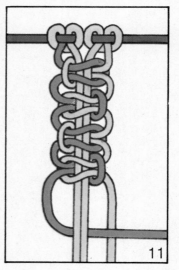

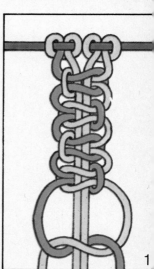

Mounting the strands

1 Fold each single strand in half and place under the handle.

2 Then take both ends over the handle and through the loop.

3 Now pull the two ends through the loop and then downward.

4 Finally, pull the knot tight. Complete the row in this way, with required number of strands.

Working the square knots

5 The knot is made of two pairs of strands. Place the left-hand strand over the two center strands and under the right-hand one.

6 Place the right-hand strand under the center strands and over the left-hand one.

7 Then place the right-hand strand over, the left-hand one under the center strands.

8 Tighten the knot, taking care to keep center strands taut.

9—12 These diagrams show you how to make square knot chains. Work square knots alternately from left to right and right to left.

13 This diagram shows the alternated square knots forming a net, and how to join the front to the back with square knots.

Side join

In macrame

String them along

Materials Required: Jute: About 150 m (163 yds). 2 circular wooden bag handles.

Making the bag

Detailed diagrams of the knots are given on the opposite page.

Cut 24 strands for the front and 24 for the back of the bag, each 3 m ($3\frac{1}{4}$ yds) long. Double the strands and knot them side by side onto the handles as shown in Figs. 1–4. It is easier to work if you hang the handles on a hook or door knob.

Divide the strands into groups of 4 and make 12 chains of square knots (Figs. 5–8) with 8 knots in each (Figs. 9–12). Then, take the first handle and work the 1st row of the net pattern: take 2 strands from each of 2 adjacent groups and make 2 square knots one below the other. Continue along the row. Work the 2nd row of square knots in staggered formation. Now begin the 2nd handle in the same way. From the 3rd row onward, join the front to the back on each side with 2 square knots on alternate rows (Fig. 13).

After about 12 rows, finish the base by knotting together 4 threads from the front and 4 from the back all the way along. Turn the net inside out so that the ends are hidden inside or trim the ends evenly and leave as a fringe.

Macrame hammock

Swinging into summer

Just below the rod, make 8 rows of 21 square knots in each of the different colored strings. The ends are bound together to suspend the hammock.

You can doze off comfortably and swing safely in this wide hammock made of strong synthetic string. It will take a fair amount of time and money to make, but will offer a lifetime of blissful relaxation.

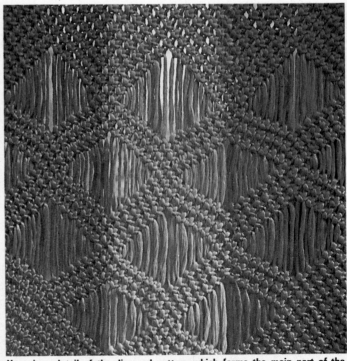

Here is a detail of the diamond pattern which forms the main part of the hammock. The diamond shapes are formed by 3 diagonal rows of square knots.

Crofts

Materials Required:

Strong synthetic string in 500 m or 550 yd balls: 2 balls green, 2 balls dark blue, 1 ball light blue. 2 solid curtain rods, each 1 m (1 yd) in length. 4 spherical rod ends. Dark blue enamel paint.

Mounting the threads

For each of the 5 stripes, measure out 32 strands of 14 m ($15\frac{1}{4}$ yds) each. To facilitate the work, wrap each strand into a butterfly bobbin by winding the strand round your finger and thumb in a figure-eight and securing with an elastic band. The strand is released by a gentle pull.

Screw the rod ends onto the rods and paint both. Suspend one of the rods from 2 nails with thick string. Leave about 2.50 m ($2\frac{3}{4}$ yds) of each strand hanging down for the suspension cords which will be worked at the end. Knot all the strands tightly onto the rod with half hitches (Diagram 1). Push all the threads close together.

Working the pattern

The main part of the hammock is worked in square knots (Diagram 2). The first 20 cm (8") consists of cords of square knots. With the first 4 strands, make 21 square knots, one below the other. Repeat with all the remaining strands (see top photograph on the previous page).

Now work 9 rows of alternated square knots: In the 1st row, make a square knot with each group of 4 strands. In the 2nd row, leave out the first 2 threads and make square knots with the following groups of 4. In the 3rd row, begin with the first 4 strands

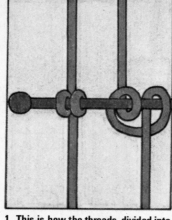

1. This is how the threads, divided into color groups, are knotted onto the rod with half hitches.

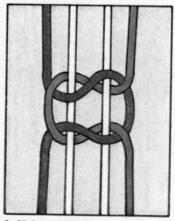

2. Make a square knot with 4 strands by tying the outer 2 around the inner 2 as shown. Pull tight.

3. Square knots can be alternated from row to row to form a staggered pattern as on the main part of the hammock.

again (Diagram 3).

In the 9th row, find the knot which is 5 knots down and 4 knots across. This is the apex of the first diamond in the pattern. Each side of a diamond has 8 knots. The shape is created by knotting

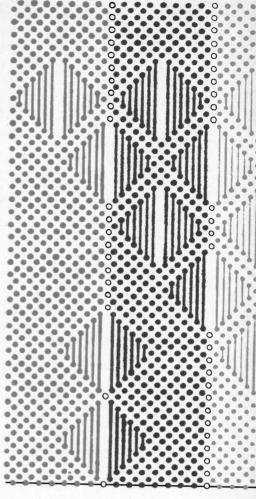

This diagram shows the first quarter of the main pattern. Repeat the pattern in reverse for the second quarter. Work the first half in reverse to make the second half.

● ● ● Square knots
○ 2-colored knots (change of color)

2 strands less from the center out in each of the following rows, leaving them hanging down. When 8 rows of knots have been worked, keep adding 2 more strands from the sides to the center in each row, pulling them taut. Work the other half of the diamond in reverse to match (see lower photograph on the previous page). Continue knotting, following the diagram at the top right, which shows a quarter of the pattern. Repeat the pattern in reverse for the 2nd quarter. When you reach the center, repeat the pattern again as a mirror image for the other half. On completion of the whole pattern, join on the rod at the other end with half hitches as before.

Working the ends

In the 1st row, gather all the strands of each color

together. At about 8 cm (3"), wrap a strand around them about 10 times. In the 2nd row, divide the bundles of strands in half and combine each bundle with the color next to it, so that the wrappings are in a staggered line from the 1st row. In the 3rd row, all the light blue threads are grouped together, and at the sides, all the green and dark blue are grouped together. In the 4th row, divide the light blue threads and join them with the green and dark blue at the sides. In the last row, all threads are wrapped together.

Trim the strand ends to 45 cm ($17\frac{3}{4}$"). Divide them into 2 bundles and overlap these by 15 cm (6") to form a ring. Bind the ring securely with a strand at least 1.5 m ($1\frac{5}{8}$ yds) long. Fasten off binding strand securely.

Index

Index

Notes

Notes

Notes

Notes